The Rainy Day BOOK

A PICK ME UP! BOOK

COUNTRYMAN ®

A Division of Thomas Nelson Publishers

Since 1798

www.thomasnelson.com

Published by J. Countryman® a division of Thomas Nelson, Inc., Nashville, Tennessee 37214

Editorial development by Mark Gilroy Communications
Managing editor: Jessica Inman

For a list of acknowledgments, see page 220.

Unless otherwise indicated, Scripture quotations are taken from The Holy Bible,
New Century Version, copyright © 1987, 1988, 1991 by Word Publishing, Dallas, Texas 75039.
Used by permission.

Scriptures marked NKJV are taken from The New King James Version.
Copyright © 1979, 1980, 1982, Thomas Nelson, Inc.

Scripture quotations marked NLT are taken from the Holy Bible, New Living Translation,
copyright © 1996. Used by permission of Tyndale House Publishers, Inc., Wheaton, Illinois 60189.
All rights reserved.

www.jcountryman.com
www.thomasnelson.com

Designed by Thinkpen Design, LLC, Springdale, Arkansas

ISBN 1404103376

Printed and bound in the United States of America

Contents

Surprise Showers 67

Thunderstorms 105

Blue Days 135

Sunshiny Days 163

Sprinkles on a Hot Day 189

Acknowledgements 220

GENTLE RAINS

Some people walk in the rain, others just get wet.

ROGER MILLER

Uh-oh. It's raining. I'm going to look like a drowned rat when I get inside the restaurant. Oh, man, I wish it could have held off another ten minutes!

Rain, even the gentle kind, is considered to be a nuisance for many of us. We dash from our car to the door, a newspaper or anything else we can lay hands on covering our head, in a vain attempt to save our neatly coifed hair.

Kids have it right. Take off your shoes, and puddles ain't so bad after all. Change into some old grubbies, and a gentle rain feels downright refreshing.

Life includes inconveniences and setbacks, but sometimes a little adversity can refresh our souls by reminding us what really matters and what's not that big of a deal.

In the following selections, including "The Double Trouble," a story that doesn't quite smell right, and "The Pope and Brad Pitt," one that is certain to inspire a smile and maybe even a guffaw from the ladies, rediscover God's ways of renewing and refreshing your spirit even when it's raining. Okay, a few boring days might be nice, but who knows what fun surprises wait for you in the days that follow!

PEOPLE WHO DO WHAT IS RIGHT MAY HAVE MANY PROBLEMS, BUT THE LORD WILL SOLVE THEM ALL.

PSALM 34:19

*People find it hard
to be both comic
and serious, though
life manages it
easily enough.*

MIGNON MCLAUGHLIN

The Double Trouble

GINGER BODA

On a steamy Friday night in mid-July, I arrived home from my swing shift just before midnight. I found my husband, Mark, asleep on the sofa (no, he wasn't in the doghouse—just dozed off watching TV). The following day was his birthday, so my youngest teen, Alisha, had baked him a beautiful cake. I frosted it and placed it on the kitchen table alongside his birthday presents, as I wanted him to be surprised in the morning. Alisha and Jason, my oldest, were also fast asleep.

I, on the other hand, was wide awake, jazzed about tomorrow's celebration. I decided to top off the birthday display with a few cut roses from our garden. Mark had become quite the gardener, so I knew he would appreciate seeing his beauties used as birthday decor. I took his brand-new rose pruners and headed out the front door. After finding a few choice blooms in our garden near the driveway, I ambled across the lawn to the other strip of bushes. Spotting a perfect red rose, I snipped it to add to the others in my hand.

At that moment, I heard a rustling noise right in front of me, but in the darkness I could only barely make out what appeared to be a huge cat. Unfortunately for me, it wasn't a cat. Almost immediately, I heard a hissing sound. As my eyes finally adjusted to the dark, I saw him standing there, only three feet in front of me, his bushy tail spread wide to pump a musky substance onto my skin. As he fired, I jumped and yelled in a voice that could shatter glass, "Skunk!"

I ran screaming across the yard toward the safety of my home. Arms flailing, I turned onto the walkway leading to our front door only to find another skunk lying in wait for me. The second intruder, only two feet away, shot me with more vigor than the first, and his aim was much more deadly. I was screaming my head off, mouth agape, when the odoriferous projectile quickly introduced itself to my taste buds. Yuck!

Of course, birthday boy awoke from his slumber when I ran into the house, and my daughter too came racing down the hallway. There I was—pruners in one hand, roses in the other, wailing, "Skunks! Skunks! I got tag teamed by two skunks!" Naturally, the smell had accompanied me into the house, and chaos set in immediately, along with some chuckles from my daughter as she frantically called a friend for help and advice.

Mark was half awake by then, trying to get his bearings while he assessed the situation. I threw down the roses and pruners and ran to the laundry area in our garage, stripped off my work clothes, tossed them into the washer set on hot, and stood there, stark naked, begging for someone to get me a towel. Mark threw me one, all the while encouraging me to "Please stay put!"

I frantically ran to the bathtub. Alisha, phone in hand, brought me cans and cans of tomato sauce to cover myself from head to toe, including my tongue and nose—ugh! I was cold, crying, and miserable. Mark was running around, hosing off the front of the house with water to dissipate the stink, wishing all the while that tomato juice could be plumbed through the pipes.

Soon, we had every fan in the house going. The fragrance of scented candles, potpourri, and air freshener mingled with the horrid skunk stench to create a truly unforgettable aroma. It was nearly 5:30 A.M.

I stood there, stark naked, begging for someone to get me a towel.

before we began to sense some relief from the horrendous experience that had befallen us. By morning, I had washed my clothes with extra fabric softener four times. I had showered off the tomato sauce, but not until I had snorted some of it up my nose several times. Then I had to snort water up my nose to get the tomato sauce out, nearly drowning myself.

Later, Alisha told me that she had to keep leaving the bathroom for fear of the nightmares she might have after seeing me choking and crying and sitting naked in the tub, covered with red tomato sauce, which looked like blood. As sympathetic as she was, though, the whole affair still seemed like an episode of *I Love Lucy*—or maybe a scene from the movie *Psycho*—and she couldn't help laughing out loud.

When I finally calmed down, I tried to get the disgusting taste out of my mouth with toothpaste, baking soda, lemons, coffee, mouthwash, and just about anything else within reach.

Exhausted, I went out onto the back patio with toweled head to sit with Mark. All of a sudden, we turned to each other and asked, "Where is Jason?" We hurried to his room and opened his door. The now all too familiar scent that had been trapped in his room hit us once again. Amazingly, he had slept through the whole thing.

Nevertheless, all is well and back to normal at the Boda homestead these days, and the events of that night are just a fleeting aroma in our minds, bringing back quite a few laughs, of course. I have since received e-mails and letters that have educated me on skunk attack prevention and treatment. I have also been nicknamed Pepe, Flower, and Stinky.

Needless to say, I shall forever watch the movie *Bambi* with a new and bitter suspicion toward that seemingly sweet, innocent little Flower. ☁

TRUST GOD ALL THE TIME. TELL HIM ALL YOUR PROBLEMS,
BECAUSE GOD IS OUR PROTECTION.

PSALM 62:8

*When God sorts out the
weather and sends rain—
Why, rain's my choice.*

JAMES WHITCOMB RILEY

May God give you plenty
of rain and good soil so
that you will have plenty
of grain and new wine.

GENESIS 27:28

Picture Perfect

JOAN CLAYTON

It was class picture day. My students looked beautiful. But as I began lining them up at the door for their pictures, the principal's voice told us over the intercom the photographer had made a mistake in booking and wouldn't be coming to our school until the next week. Among the groans, one little girl, dressed in ruffles, her curls precisely arranged, exclaimed, "Oh, no! I took a bath for nothing!"

When it rains on your
parade, look up
rather than down.
Without the rain,
there would be
no rainbow.

G.K. CHESTERTON

The Pope and Brad Pitt

MIGNON MURRELL

I recently had to stay in the hospital for several days following an operation. It was an operation that I didn't want, but my doctor assured me was necessary. The procedure went well, and afterwards I was left to recuperate in a room that could have rivaled any four-star hotel.

"Honey, look," my husband, Bill, said excitedly as I lay in a morphine-induced stupor. "They have a lazy boy and digital cable—we're never leaving."

To ease my discomfort, I was given extra doses of morphine and unlimited access to the design channel. As the week wore on, I spiraled in and out of consciousness, greeting visitors who stopped by to wish me well and ask where Bill was. In fact, to this day, I remember the very first words I heard coming out of surgery.

Calling to me across the fog of amnesia, I heard the sound of my pastor's voice, "Hi, Mignon," he said. "Where's Bill?" It was then that I knew I had survived and was now back in the real world.

Never mind the fact that I have never met Brad Pitt or even knew anyone who knew him. The fact that he was nice enough to come to the hospital to visit was good enough for me.

During my weeklong stay, I began to grow depressed. Several friends dropped by to chat and cheer me up. Some of them I do not remember, and some of them I will never forget. Like the day Brad Pitt came by. He walked into the room holding a bundle of the most beautiful flowers I'd ever seen.

"Why, Brad," I said, trying to sit up taller in my bed as I adjusted my flimsy, paper-thin gown (there is just no dignity in a hospital). "What are you doing here?"

"Well, Mignon," he replied with a flash of that famous boyish grin, "I heard that you were in the hospital, and I had a break from filming, so I thought I would drop by."

I am so sorry, Father, that I cannot get out of bed and kiss your ring," I said, awed by his presence. He continued to pray over me, telling me that I would get well and not to lose heart. I continued to feel bad about not getting out of the bed; after all, the Pope was praying for me!

Never mind the fact that I have never met Brad Pitt nor even knew anyone who knew him. The fact that he was nice enough to stop by the hospital to visit was good enough for me. We talked on and on about various things that I can't recall, but one thing I do remember was the speed with which he left. One minute he was there, and when I turned my head to get a drink of water he was gone.

I was not alone for long, because shortly after, in walked none other than Pope John Paul II himself. My surgery occurred when he was still alive. He looked powerful and dazzling in his white regalia and pointy hat. He waved his hand toward me, making the sign of the cross.

"I am so sorry, Father, that I cannot get out of bed and kiss your ring," I said, awed by his presence. He continued to pray over me, telling me that I would get well and not to lose heart. I continued to feel bad about not getting out of the bed; after all, the Pope was praying for me! Our visit was cut short, however, when I turned to slide out of the bed so that I could kneel. When I looked up, he was gone.

Now, up to this point I had not thought it all strange that a movie star and a religious dignitary should visit me, an average thirty-five-year-old Protestant located in a hospital in southern Texas. But as I sat there, the truth slowly dawned on me. In my morphine-induced state I was having hallucinations—wild ones. I laughed out loud. God sure did have a sense of humor. My friends still ask me what was on my mind before the surgery.

Here I had been feeling sorry for myself, alone and unable to pray— yet the Lord had sent me two imaginary emissaries to lighten my load and reassure me that He was still there. Even though it was a strange way to do it, the Lord used the incident to lift my mood and focus my attention back onto Him with gratitude.

The memory of that hospital stay turned out to be another opportunity to see God's faithfulness and support working in my life. Though I have to say, I sure miss talking with Brad Pitt. ☁

YOUR FATHER KNOWS THE THINGS
YOU NEED BEFORE YOU ASK HIM.
MATTHEW 6:8

They Said It

Anyone who says sunshine brings
happiness has never danced in the rain.

AUTHOR UNKNOWN

We may run, walk, stumble, drive, or fly, but let us never
lose sight of the reason for the journey, or miss
a chance to see a rainbow on the way.

GLORIA GAITHER

The way I see it, if you want the rainbow,
you gotta put up with the rain.

DOLLY PARTON

If you don't know about pain and trouble, you're in sad shape.
They make you appreciate life.

EVEL KNIEVEL

If you don't go fishing because you thought it might rain
you will never go fishing. This applies to more than fishing.

GARY SOW

Sunshine is delicious, rain is refreshing, wind braces us up,
snow is exhilarating; there is really no such thing as bad weather,
only different kinds of good weather.

JOHN RUSKIN

Who Sends the Rain?

As long has there have been raindrops, people have wondered where they came from. Even the ancients posted theories on the origin of rain.

In Aristophanes' *The Clouds*, Socrates declares that rain does not, in fact, come directly from Zeus, but rather, rain and thunder come when "the Clouds, when full of rain, bump against one another, and that, being inordinately swollen out, they burst with a great noise."

Aristotle says, "Now the sun, moving as it does, sets up processes of change and becoming and decay, and by its agency the finest and sweetest water is every day carried up and is dissolved into vapor and rises to the upper region, where it is condensed again by the cold and so returns to the earth."

Maybe the rain in your life doesn't feel like "the finest and sweetest water." But rest assured that God is in control of all things. As another ancient thinker put it, "He fills the sky with clouds and sends rain to the earth and makes grass grow on the hills" (Psalm 147:8).

A good friend is cheaper than therapy and much more fun.

ANONYMOUS

Dancing on Potato Chips

CHRISTY PHILLIPPE

Recently I had one of those days. Everything went wrong—including my plans for dinner. I should have stopped by the market, but I was too frazzled. Surely there'd be something to eat at home.

Seeing that my cupboard was barer than I remembered, I opted for soup. I had a can open and in the saucepan before I realized we were out of milk. Plan B was leftover baked beans, but that idea was nixed when I saw that the container was growing a healthy crop of mold.

In desperation, I grabbed a bag of potato chips. Pulling hard on the plastic corners, I struggled to open the easy-open bag, and suddenly, I did. The bag split, and the chips flew sky high.

My cry of anguish was heard in the living room. My roommate, who had just returned home, rushed in and did the most helpful thing she could think of—and just what I needed. She jumped into the middle of the pile of chips and started dancing!

Tired of feeling sorry for myself, I let out a laugh and started dancing too. As we foxtrotted over potato chip crumbs, I was grateful for a friend to help me dance away the discouragements and inconveniences of life. ☁

Laughter is a tranquilizer with no side effects.

ARNOLD GLASOW

Keep Them Laughing

KAYLEEN J. REUSSER

I refused to take another step. Our family of five had trekked around San Francisco for five days on foot (the trolleys were always full), and my legs felt like lead. My husband was tired too, but he wanted us to hike Muir Woods before we left for home the next day.

Looking at the faces of our eleven- and thirteen-year-old, I could tell they weren't enthusiastic about going up yet another hill either. Wondering how we could solve this situation while keeping everyone happy—no small feat for any family—I glanced over at our youngest.

Eight-year-old Lindsay jumped to the front of our pack, brandishing a walking stick as a baton. "Thanks for tuning in to the Lunge Lindsay aerobics class," she announced. "Today we will hike to the top of this mountain. Just put one foot in front of the other, folks, and follow me!" Then she turned around and began climbing.

> To this day, we still chuckle about how "Lunge Lindsay" got the family to climb that mountain together.

The rest of us, too startled to think, followed.

Lindsay's continued fitness-expert antics were so hysterical that we laughed throughout the rest of the hike. To this day, we still chuckle about how "Lunge Lindsay" got the family to climb that mountain together.

In his book *The Seven Habits of Highly Effective Families*, Stephen Covey, father of nine, says this about family humor: "In our family the central element that has preserved the sanity, fun, unity, togetherness, and magnetic attraction of our family culture is laughter—telling jokes, seeing the 'funny' side of life, poking holes at stuffed shirts, and simply having fun together." Laughter and fun make family life a pleasure and lighten our loads.

Keep in mind that what one family finds humorous or fun to do together, another might not. The secret is to be alert and sensitive to personalities and interests.

One of our family favorites is to watch funny old movies together, like Abbott and Costello routines and *Arsenic and Old Lace*. Another is to cut out comics and place them on the fridge for everyone to share ("Family Circus" is a perennial hit in our house). I have also snapped photos of the kids when they are doing something silly, like trying on Grandma's old hats and gloves and pretending they are "grown-up," and displayed the photos around the house to give each room a special "funny" memory.

By doing these things, my husband and I hope to raise cheerful kids who are full of good stories, whom other people want to be around.

But humor also holds benefits for physical health. Mental health professionals know that people who laugh at their mistakes recover faster from illness than perfectionists. The Bible says, "A happy heart is like good medicine" (Proverbs 17:22).

Chuck Swindoll, father of four, affirms the effect of humor on a person's mental health in his book *Home: Where Life Makes Up Its Mind*: "Laughter is the most beautiful and beneficial therapy God ever granted humanity."

In our family, humor has healed rifts before they became destructive chasms.

One night, ten-year-old Chris had pushed my last button. I wanted to give him a lecture that began with, "How many times have I told you not to do that!" and lasted well into the night. I also wanted to punch something, but I knew that probably wouldn't help the situation.

Finally, I stood up straight, shook my finger at him, and warned, "If you don't behave, I'll...tickle your toes!"

After a brief pause, my onlooking daughters started laughing. I joined them, feeling much better than I would have had I given in to my natural impulses. Chris smiled faintly, surprised by my response, but obviously relieved. He even started behaving better—for a while, anyway.

My threat of the torture of tickling has become famous around our house. In fact, my kids often tell their friends about it, guffawing each time. It doesn't bother me. Laughter makes family life fun in spite of the struggles we sometimes encounter, and hearing my kids laugh is a gift, almost sacred. ☁

A HAPPY HEART IS LIKE GOOD MEDICINE,
BUT A BROKEN SPIRIT DRAINS YOUR STRENGTH.

PROVERBS 17:22

Rain in Summer

HENRY WADSWORTH LONGFELLOW

How beautiful is the rain!
After the dust and heat,
In the broad and fiery street,
In the narrow lane,
How beautiful is the rain!

How it clatters along the roofs,
Like the tramp of hoofs!
How it gushes and struggles out
From the throat of the overflowing spout!

Across the windowpane
It pours and pours;
And swift and wide,
With a muddy tide,
Like a river down the gutter roars
The rain, the welcome rain!

Job Jar

In the classic "Hi and Lois" comic strip, Lois keeps a jar of chores for Hi to accomplish on Saturdays—preferably before golf outings with his neighbor, Thirsty. For fifty years, this has been a nice setup for some gag lines, particularly in relation to Thirsty, who works very hard at doing nothing all day.

There is some truth to the old advice that one way to feel better is to get something accomplished. Create a rainy-day task jar. Write on slips of paper some chores you want to get done but never get around to: organizing CDs; pulling too-small and worn out clothes from the kids' closets and drawers; polishing woodwork or fixtures; cleaning and organizing garage shelves.

Next time it rains, stick your hand in the job jar and do whatever chore comes up. It may not sound like a ton of fun, but you'll feel better! ☁

A Rainbow and a Promise

GENESIS 9

Rainbows are so common in popular designs and illustrations that it's easy to forget that the rainbow is a sacred symbol in the Bible, with the same powerful force as other "marks" of God's graciousness. It appears at the end of the account of the Great Flood (Genesis 6-8), and it commemorated God's promise to Noah that "Floods will never again destroy all life on the earth" (Genesis 9:15).

Some biblical scholars have debated whether the Great Flood denoted a seismic change in the earth's atmosphere—"On the seventeenth day of the second month of that year the underground springs split open, and the clouds in the sky poured out rain" (Genesis 7:11)—which included the advent of rain and rainbows. After all, the fall was so pervasive and awful that it even affected the earth: "Against its will, everything on earth was subjected to God's curse" (Romans 8:20 NLT).

Rainbows are ultimately a reminder of God's love for His children—

💧 "But God's mercy is great, and he loved us very much. Though we were spiritually dead because of the things we did against God, he gave us new life with Christ. You have been saved by God's grace" (Ephesians 2:4-5).

💧 "I love you people with a love that will last forever. That is why I have continued showing you kindness" (Jeremiah 31:3).

💧 "The Father has loved us so much that we are called children of God. And we really are his children" (I John 3:1).

💧 "But God shows his great love for us in this way: Christ died for us while we were still sinners" (Romans 5:8). ☁

God's Promises
for Life's Little Troubles

God will...

Take on your life's battles

*The Lord says this to you: "Don't be afraid
or discouraged because of this large army.
The battle is not your battle, it is God's."*

2 CHRONICLES 20:15

Help you face problems

*The Lord helps those who have been defeated
and takes care of those who are in trouble.*

PSALM 145:14

Give you peace
The Lord gives strength to his people;
the Lord blesses his people with peace.

PSALM 29:11

Give you everything you need
The Lord is my shepherd;
I have everything I need.

PSALM 23:1

Use your circumstances to bless you
We know that in everything God works
for the good of those who love him.

ROMANS 8:28

A Prayer of Praise and Thanksgiving

Dear Heavenly Father,

I know that You know just what I need—and You have always met my needs with such faithfulness, Lord. You give so many good gifts. Help me remember that You are the Creator and Sustainer of everything, Lord God. Thank You that You have bent down near to me and allowed me to glimpse Your presence in my life.

With all my breath, I will express my worship, my gratitude, and my needs to You today.

OVERCAST DAYS

Never think that God's delays are God's denials.
Hold on; hold fast; hold out. Patience is genius.

GEORGES-LOUIS LECLERC BUFFON

Can't tell what it's going to do today. Wish the weather would make up its mind. Now I can't decide whether to wash the car—which would guarantee rain—and then go for a family picnic (another surefire rain-maker), or just plan to stay inside and catch up on paperwork and reading.

One of the most sincere prayers ever prayed is the humorous cry, "Dear Lord, grant me patience, and please grant it right now."

On those days when you're waiting for something good to happen—or just anything to happen—it's good to remember that there's a rhythm to life that requires waiting. Read this section carefully and you'll find some encouraging words from the movie *Jaws*. Don't miss "Rushin' Roulette," a reminder of how good stillness can be, and follow it up with "Are We There Yet?" You'll for sure look forward to a slow, lazy season of life—even if you don't have all the answers.

IT IS SAD NOT TO GET WHAT YOU HOPED FOR. BUT WISHES THAT
COME TRUE ARE LIKE EATING FRUIT FROM THE TREE OF LIFE.

PROVERBS 13:12

*Slow down and enjoy life.
It's not only the scenery
you miss by going too
fast—you also miss the
sense of where you are
going and why.*

EDDIE CANTOR

Are We There Yet?

PATT HARPER

We had only been on the road an hour, with seven very long hours to go, when the query was first uttered: "Are we there yet?" The biggest surprise was that it came from me, the assumed adult. We were en route to visit my sister and her husband, and I couldn't wait to chat with her over pots of coffee, spend hours shopping for nothing in particular, and laugh into the wee hours of the night. I was not, however, looking forward to being on that boring stretch of interstate for a third of a day.

As I began to repeat my mantra, my husband took an unexpected turn onto an exit ramp. I immediately flashbacked to my childhood when my father would pull over and soundly scold me for whining, and sheepishly asked Dale if something were wrong. He grinned his most mischievous grin and announced that we were going to take the back roads.

Less than fifteen minutes later, he howled, "Look, Patt—turkeys!" There in the ditch alongside the road were three toms strutting in the glow of the sunrise.

He continued to point out wildlife and unusual landforms as we drove along. Often we would take an unscripted detour to check out a small-town museum, a historical marker, or one of those must-see out-of-the-way attractions. The normally grueling eight-hour trip took an astonishingly short ten hours.

Our visit was as magnificent as I had expected. But as our time together came to a close, I once again faced that dismal trek down the interstate. Without the luxury of time we'd had on the first leg of our journey, I knew we had no choice but to forego the lively back roads in favor of the boring highway.

He grinned his most mischievous grin and announced that we were going to take the back roads.

As the suitcase closed with a thud, Dale asked if I had packed the book my sister had just given him, the historical epic *Black Elk Speaks* by John G. Niehardt. He wanted me to read it to him on the way home. Stunned, I asked if he meant for me to read it out loud. He replied that he'd have a hard time hearing it if I read it to myself.

The trip home was amazing. I would read a chapter, and then we would absorb its content and discuss its significance. Dale would often awe me with the breadth of his knowledge of Native American folklore.

That vacation was not only one of my favorites, but also an epiphany for me. I had always set my sights on a goal and viewed the steps between as merely necessary evils. However, there on that long highway, I learned that the journey could and should be as important and enjoyable as the destination. Now, whether I'm traveling or working toward a goal, I don't ask, "Are we there yet?" Instead, I enjoy the ride! ☁

TODAY IS A HOLY DAY TO THE LORD.

NEHEMIAH 8:10

They Said It

The trick is to experience each moment with a clear mind and an open
heart. When you do that, the game—and life—will take care of itself.

PHIL JACKSON

Having spent the better part of my life trying either to relive
the past or experience the future before it arrives, I have come
to believe that in between these two extremes is peace.

AUTHOR UNKNOWN

Make each day your masterpiece.

JOHN WOODEN

The living moment is everything.

D.H. LAWRENCE

The other day a man asked me what I thought was the best time of life.
"Why," I answered without a thought, "now."

DAVID GRAYSON

God made the world round so we would never
be able to see too far down the road.

ISAK DINESEN

Don't be fooled by the calendar.
There are only as many days in the year as you make use of.

CHARLES RICHARDS

God turns the ordinary into the extraordinary.

ERWIN TIPPEL

No yesterdays are
ever wasted for those
who give themselves
to today.

BRENDAN FRANCIS

A Friend in Need

NANCY B. GIBBS

In her first days of retirement, Betty went into a period of depression. She lost her feelings of self-worth. She saw a counselor, but nothing seemed to lift her out of her deep, black pit of misery.

Then one dismal Sunday afternoon she happened to be looking at a copy of her church's membership roll, noting the names of women who had recently become widows. *Haven't seen them at church lately*, Betty noted. *Why don't you visit them?* said a small voice from within.

Betty wrote their names and addresses on a card, put on her coat, and headed out. At the first house, she found a woman alone, confused, and in need of medical attention. Betty, no longer despondent, took charge of the situation. Her depression disappeared immediately.

Almost instantaneously she began to thrive again, knowing she had a purpose and was following God's plan for her life. ☁

Joke Break

You might not laugh at these jokes unless you're, say, seven years old. But everyone needs a few moments of pure silly, a break from the humdrum every now and then. Let these jokes remind you that there's something funny to be found even in blah, boring days.

"Hello, may I speak to the principal, please?"
"This is the principle."
"I'm calling to say that my son cannot come
to school today because he has a bad cold."
"Who is this speaking, please?"
"This is my father."

What did the bored cow say as she got up in the morning?
"Just an udder day."

What happens when the sun gets tired?
It sets awhile.

Patience

RUTH COWLES

I asked the Lord for patience
    I know I need it so.
When I put in a garden,
    I can't wait for it to grow.

I cannot wait for mail to come,
    Pots to boil, bread to rise,
For friends to call or write or visit,
    Sun to burst through stormy skies.

I know to be impatient
    Is a sin, akin to worry.
So, I asked the Lord for patience.
    I just wish that He would hurry!

*What's the use
of hurrying when there's
a perfectly good day
coming tomorrow
that hasn't even
been touched?*

AUTHOR UNKNOWN

Rushin' Roulette

CINDY L. HEFLIN

I slapped the snooze bar and rolled over to steal a few more moments of sleep. *But it's Saturday*, my body pleaded as a beam of sunlight pierced the darkened room, poking me in the eye. Heaving a sigh, I reluctantly threw off the covers and crawled out of bed.

Still slightly comatose, I stumbled past my husband's unpacked luggage and into the shower. While the steamy spray pummeled my scalp, the day's busy schedule swirled inside my head. I quickly hurled several prayers heavenward, promising I'd get around to having some quiet time with God a little later.

I pulled on a pair of sweats, dashed downstairs to the kitchen, and tossed a bowl of cereal to each kid. While they sat at the island crunching on Crispix, my husband, Bryant, and I checked our mile-long to-do list.

"How about a picnic in the park for lunch?" I suggested, hoping to carve out some family time in the middle of our hectic day. My gang was up for it, but a severe storm in the forecast soon dampened our outdoor plans. Playing it safe, we opted to catch the newest kid-flick at a nearby cinema.

"What if I cook, clean up the house, and finish party preparations while you shuttle the girls to softball, dance class, and take the dog to the vet," I offered. "Then we could run errands together and squeeze the movie in before Grandma's birthday party."

THE RAINY DAY BOOK

"Okay, girls. Let's go!" Bryant called as the kids scrambled out the door to our sky-blue minivan. While he taxied our cherubs all over town, I tackled the chores at home. Fun and frantic—just an ordinary Saturday.

As time raced by, I hurried to clean the countertops, clearing away dirty dishes, star-spangled school papers, a slimy science fair project, and a myriad of books. Feeling a twinge of guilt, I idly thumbed the pages of my daily devotional before placing it on the table with a pile of mail. My heart longed for a peaceful moment of God's presence, but the tyrannous clock was ticking.

Sheer terror overwhelmed me when I saw the strange man seated behind the wheel of the van. Concluding that Bryant and the girls were missing, my mind wildly raced through all the horrible possibilities.

After crossing off each item on my checklist, I made a beeline for the bedroom to change clothes and pop in my contacts. Soon, the honking horn in my driveway jolted me—our errands! I scurried from room to room like a squirrel gathering nuts before winter, collecting library books, dry cleaning, and an overdue video. Checking our bedside clock, I glanced at my Bible with a brief sigh before hustling out to the van, juggling a cumbersome load in my arms.

"Just three little errands before the movie, remember?" I sighed, dumping the heap into my lap.

"Aw, Mom!" the backseat chorused.

Through the afternoon drizzle, we raced the clock, rushing to finish our rounds before showtime. Since he'd just returned after yet another week of business travel, we made use of our time between stops, bringing Dad up to speed on family concerns and school activities.

"So what'd you learn about this week?" he asked each child.

"Stranger-Danger!" said our six-year-old confidently. My husband shot a questioning look my way.

"Safety Week at school," I explained with a smile. "First graders read a booklet learning rules about crossing the street, riding the bus, and avoiding strangers."

Windshield wipers slurping, we continued our "family time," cruising the rain-slick streets to our last stop.

Halfway through dismantling an urgent family issue, we arrived at the video store. Sudden thunder crashed overhead as Bryant parked at the curb by the door and I rushed in with our overdue tape. To allow the vehicle behind him access to the entrance, my ever-courteous husband moved ahead a few car lengths. The other driver pulled up immediately, and parked his vehicle—a sky-blue van identical to ours—in the space we had just occupied.

I buzzed through the busy store straight to the counter, paid the fee, and headed back. With the grace and speed of a crazed gazelle, I swept by the bargain aisle, squelching my proclivity to browse, and maneuvered my way through a maze of shoppers.

Reaching the van, I flung open the door, dropped into my seat, and promptly continued our discussion, never skipping a beat. *Why isn't he driving on to the theater?* I wondered, when I noticed something odd rolling around at my feet. Puzzled, I picked up the fuzzy, fluorescent green sphere. "Where'd this tennis ball come from?" I asked, turning toward the driver's seat as I casually tossed the ball over my shoulder.

"Mommy?" my concerned first-grader cried over the din of laughter. With fear in her voice and tears in her eyes, she was visibly shaken. "Don't you remember? It's not safe to get in a stranger's car!"

Sheer terror overwhelmed me when I saw the strange man seated behind the wheel of the van. Concluding that Bryant and the girls were missing, my mind wildly raced through all the horrible possibilities. I didn't know whether to pray first or scream. A dead silence hung in the air. Totally numb, I sat there frozen with fear, like a deer in the headlights. *Come to think of it, this guy looks pretty shocked too...*

Staring out the windshield, I suddenly saw another blue minivan parked straight ahead in front of the next store. Without a word, I bolted out the door and dashed in the rain down the sidewalk. Relief and embarrassment washed over me as I realized my family was safe inside.

Safe—and completely oblivious to my close and unexpected encounter. My heart still pounding, I described the ordeal in full detail. Bryant listened with an astonished gaze, and suddenly we all exploded with laughter. Tears rolling down our cheeks, we howled until our sides ached and wondered if that poor man was amused too, or just plain shocked.

"Mommy?" my concerned first-grader cried over the din of laughter. With fear in her voice and tears in her eyes, she was visibly shaken. "Don't you remember? It's not safe to get in a stranger's car!"

After consoling our daughter, we thanked God for His divine protection and raced to the movie.

My nerves calmed as I collapsed into a seat in the darkened theater. Soon, my heart overflowed with the peace of God's presence, as a comforting voice whispered, "Be still, My child, and know that I am God." A moment of quiet punctuated my frenzied day, reminding me to thank God for His presence in the midst of chaos—and for those quiet days I so often take for granted! ☁

BE STILL, AND KNOW THAT I AM GOD.
PSALM 46:10 NKJV

Give us, Lord, a bit o' sun,
A bit o' work and a bit o' fun;
Give us all in the struggle and sputter
Our daily bread and a bit o' butter.

ENGLISH PRAYER

A Retro Read

As a kid, I spent a sizable chunk of my Saturdays at the public library. I brought home armfuls of books—horse care manuals, stories about the Loch Ness Monster, Civil War biographies, tales of the escapades of ultra-cool high school girls.

If your Saturday is looking gloomy, maybe an old-fashioned, unhurried trip to the library is in order. Revisit great childhood reads like *Charlotte's Web* and *Tales of a Fourth Grade Nothing*. A lot of libraries have a substantial stock of music CDs—some cheer-me-up suggestions: Motown classics, early Beach Boys albums, good jazz, or whatever you listened to as a teenager. You might even visit the video section and pick out a classic Charlie Brown cartoon or a favorite holiday movie.

Who knows—maybe a few hours of reminiscent browsing as you celebrate today will turn your blah Saturday into a bright one.

Normal day, let me be aware
of the treasure you are.
Let me learn from you, love you,
bless you before you depart.
Let me not pass you by in quest
of some rare and perfect tomorrow.
Let me hold you while I may,
for it may not always be so.
One day I shall dig my nails
into the earth, or bury my face
in the pillow, or stretch myself taut,
or raise my hands to the sky and want,
more than all the world, your return.

MARY JEAN IRON

*God gives us dreams
a size too big so that
we can grow in them.*

AUTHOR UNKNOWN

The Boy Who Liked to Play with Trains

HEATHER LYNN IVESTER

My two-year-old son, Peter, ambled into our bedroom, clutching his favorite train tightly to his chest. The blue plastic Thomas the Tank Engine is Peter's constant companion, traveling with him to the sand box and the grocery store and on his various naptime adventures. He pushes the little train, lips puckered to form "choo-choo" sounds as he chugs along the carpeted floor.

Upstairs, his room is covered in a set of wooden tracks where he and his older brother form amazing worlds that are as real to them as my laundry piles are to me. There's something magical to them about watching engines pull cars along tracks in a kingdom of their own making.

I'm reminded of a story of another boy who loved playing with his Lionel train set. He inventively set up his trains in daring scenarios that involved imaginary people and simple but clever storylines. The characters came alive in his imagination, and were too

He kept playing his game of pretend, watching and learning from those around him. Ten years later, he made a movie that released one fateful summer. To everyone's surprise, the film grossed nearly $500 million.

fantastic to be kept in his own mind. So he found an eight-millimeter camera and began filming his scenes to make home movies.

He couldn't wait to show others his action-packed films, so he got his sister to make popcorn and invited friends to watch his train shows.

As a teenager, he struggled through regular school. He was placed in a learning-disabled class until his family moved to a new school system. He barely made it to graduation. Still, he kept thinking about how much fun he had directing those train movies.

He applied to film school, but was turned down. Still, he kept on dreaming.

One day, he visited Universal Studios and loved the atmosphere. He made a new friend and wanted to spend more time looking around. So he borrowed his father's briefcase to carry lunch, dressed in a dark suit, and strode boldly into the studio. To the world, he was a nobody. But in his mind, he was an aspiring director.

He kept playing his game of pretend, watching and learning from those around him. Ten years later, he made a movie that released one fateful summer. To everyone's surprise, the film grossed nearly $500 million.

The title? *Jaws*. Directed by Steven Spielberg.

What about you? As a child, what did you dream of becoming when you grew up? Sometimes our long-buried dreams only need unearthing before they can become reality. Like tiny seeds planted into fertile soil, our visions may need a fresh dose of water and sunshine to grow. We may need to start imagining again, like we did as children. "Imagination will often carry us to worlds that never were," said astronomer Carl Sagan. "But without it we go nowhere."

In my adult life, I sometimes find myself playing pretend. After the birth of my first child, I felt like I was playing a new game. After long hours of labor, my midwife handed me a blanket-wrapped infant who stared at me with blue eyes that blinked in wisdom. To him, I was the voice he recognized from months in my womb—his mother.

Yet I didn't feel capable of suddenly morphing into somebody's mom. I felt like an actress playing a role. When my son was hungry, I fed him. When he needed a change of diapers, I took care of him. I watched his quiet body while he slept, eyes closed, breathing in and out. I took him for strolls around the neighborhood and sang lullabies to him in his room. Slowly, I developed into my role as his mother. By walking the thin line of fantasy and reality, I eventually crossed over. And now I actually feel like a mom.

> We are the house under construction, the lump of clay that God is shaping. We're never still, never stuck, never stagnant. No matter where we are now, our dreams and our faith can shape us to become something greater.

The incubator for our dreams is that deep place within our hearts, where nobody knows our secret longings. Yet there is Someone we can share with who won't laugh at our far-fetched hopes. Through prayer, we can place our visions in His hands. In Jeremiah 18:6, God says, "You are in my hands like the clay in the potter's hands." We are the house under construction, the lump of clay that God is shaping. We're never still, never stuck, never stagnant. No matter where we are now, our dreams and our faith can shape us to become something greater.

A boy playing with a train set and a camera may not look all that impressive. But with a little dreaming, a dose of imagination, and a few years of time, who knows what seed of greatness may emerge from that long, uninterrupted game of pretend. ☁

GOD BEGAN DOING A GOOD WORK IN YOU,
AND I AM SURE HE WILL CONTINUE IT UNTIL IT IS
FINISHED WHEN JESUS CHRIST COMES AGAIN.

PHILIPPIANS 1:6

Light Shining Out of Darkness

WILLIAM COWPER

God moves in a mysterious way,
His wonders to perform;
He plants His footsteps in the sea,
And rides upon the storm.

Deep in unfathomable mines
Of never failing skill,
He treasures up His bright designs,
And works His sovereign will.

Ye fearful saints, fresh courage take,
The clouds ye so much dread
Are big with mercy, and shall break
In blessings on your head.

Judge not the Lord by feeble sense,
But trust Him for His grace;
Behind a frowning providence
He hides a smiling face.

His purposes will ripen fast,
Unfolding every hour;
The bud may have a bitter taste
But sweet will be the flower.

Blind unbelief is sure to err,
And scan His work in vain;
God is His own interpreter,
And He will make it plain.

THE PRESENT MOMENT IS SIGNIFICANT,
NOT AS THE BRIDGE BETWEEN PAST AND FUTURE,
BUT BY REASON OF ITS CONTENTS, WHICH CAN
FILL OUR EMPTINESS AND BECOME OURS,
IF WE ARE CAPABLE OF RECEIVING THEM.

DAG HAMMARSKJOLD

A Thick Darkness

GENESIS 15:1-15

Abraham, the man who is known as "the father of faith," not only for Christians but for Jews and Muslims as well, was given two promises by God: first, that he would take possession of a land, and second, that he would be the father of not just a son, but of many nations.

Abraham begins a historic journey with all the faith and optimism in the world. But as the years pass, he and his wife, Sarah, still have no children and, though very wealthy, own no land of their own. The father of faith begins to worry and lose heart.

He calls out to God, "Lord God, how can I be sure that I will own this land?" (Genesis 15:8). He also argues with God, "I have no son, so my slave Eliezer from Damascus will get everything I own after I die" (Genesis 15:2). Isn't it impossible to found a nation without children and land? No wonder when he goes to sleep that night, he feels "a very terrible darkness" (Genesis 15:12).

That same night, God appears to Abraham in a dream and in a swirl of ancient pageantry and images—animal sacrifices, a mysterious fire pot and torch, solemn words of an everlasting oath—gives Abraham the ultimate assurance that He, Jehovah, the Creator God, can be trusted. In the simple message, "If I fail to do what I said I would do, may this be done unto me," He foreshadows and promises the coming of a Savior, who will pay the price for fallen humanity: God himself will take the place of the animals sacrificed.

Do you have questions for God right now? Do you wonder about your promise of a child and land? Do you feel a certain darkness that clouds your vision and even your faith?

The good news is that God will meet you and provide for you what you most need and do for you what you can't accomplish yourself. ☁

FAITH MEANS BEING SURE OF THE THINGS
WE HOPE FOR AND KNOWING THAT SOMETHING
IS REAL EVEN IF WE DO NOT SEE IT.

HEBREWS 11:1

God's Promises
for Seasons of Waiting

God will...

Fulfill His plans for your life
There are many plans in a man's heart,
Nevertheless the Lord's counsel-that will stand.

PROVERBS 19:21 NKJV

Give you strength as you wait for Him
But those who wait on the LORD will find new strength.
They will fly high on wings like eagles.
They will run and not grow weary.
They will walk and not faint.

ISAIAH 40:31 NLT

Help you make decisions
Are there those who respect the Lord?
He will point them to the best way.

PSALM 25:12

Give you peace as you trust Him
You, Lord, give true peace to those who
depend on you, because they trust you.

ISAIAH 26:3

Keep His promises
The Lord will keep all his promises of good things for you.
1 SAMUEL 25:30

Honor and reward your obedience
Obey my laws and rules; a person who
obeys them will live because of them.
LEVITICUS 18:5

Help you know what to do
Do not change yourselves to be like the
people of this world, but be changed
within by a new way of thinking.
Then you will be able to decide what
God wants for you; you will know what is good
and pleasing to him and what is perfect.
ROMANS 12:2

Give your life a sense of purpose
It is God who saved us and chose us to live a holy life.
He did this not because we deserved it, but because
that was his plan long before the world began—
to show his love and kindness to us through Christ Jesus.
2 TIMOTHY 1:9 NLT

A Prayer of Trust and Faith

Dear Heavenly Father,

There are areas in my life that don't feel very peaceful right now—I want to be and do so much more, but sometimes I get bogged down in the day-to-day and start to worry and wonder where You are.

Lord, I know that You have plans for my life. And I know that the greatest thing I could ever pursue is to know You more. Thank You that when I put my focus back on Jesus, peace follows, and I find joy and contentment.

Dear God, Your gifts truly are the best.

Thank You for the gift of today.

SURPRISE SHOWERS

God doesn't always smooth the path,
but sometimes He puts springs in the wagon.

MARSHALL LUCAS

I can't believe it. I just paid off my credit card bill, and what happens? The car breaks down and I suddenly have a bill for over a thousand bucks, and, of course, my credit card is no longer paid off. The only thing normal about my life is that it's never normal. I'm ready for life to follow a plan!

It's been said that the only thing that stays the same is change. Yes, we can draw courage from the reality that God is "the same yesterday, today, and forever" (Hebrews 13:8), but life is filled with surprises—some wonderful, some tough.

Maybe that's the way God created life to be. If everything was predictable, not only would life get awfully boring, but we would never have opportunity to stretch our wings of faith to soar.

If you like to eat apple pie, but not bake it, you'll enjoy "Apple Pie Angel" in the following pages. The story, "It's All in the Attitude" somehow finds humor in a funeral home—and in the Bible study we discover that the weather has always been the topic of the day.

I CAN DO ALL THINGS THROUGH CHRIST,
BECAUSE HE GIVES ME STRENGTH.
PHILIPPIANS 4:13

*If we give our
whole life to God,
holding nothing back
He will give His whole
life to us, holding
nothing back.*

SAM HANEY

Apple Pie Angel

KATHERINE J. CRAWFORD

Apple pie! She wants apple pie!" I sloshed dishes through hot water while moaning to my friend on the telephone. "I learn to decorate the most beautiful cake and execute a moist, melt-in-your mouth frosting, and she wants apple pie. I can't manage a decent crust, much less afford apples in Colorado Springs. They cost two arms and four legs. Not at all like buying apples in Washington."

After the mornings chores were finished, I lit into my piano practice, banging out my frustrations with chords and scales. Near ten, the phone rang.

An hour earlier, I'd offered our daughter her choice of menu for her birthday. A few unexpected expenses had destroyed our budget that October, but we were determined to hold tight to one of our few family traditions: The birthday child would choose the menu.

"Honey, when your father is paid, we'll plan for a special celebration dinner. What would you like?"

Kathy Ann counted off her wishes on her fingers like she'd dreamed of this meal for weeks. "Fried chicken, mashed potatoes, and most of all I want an apple pie."

Apple pie? I groaned inwardly.

I smiled and wished her a happy birthday as she left for school.

The second the door closed behind her, I started the dishes and called Pauline, another college wife facing a stretched budget. She suggested several solutions—none of them workable.

"Try a Bisquick crust."

"Yuck."

"Have you used oil and water?"

"Yep. Tough as shoe leather."

"Well, I guess you should start practicing. Do you have flour?"

"I've got flour—no shortening."

"Go buy a pie."

"No, that won't do. They cost too much, for one thing. They taste bad, for another."

"You better hold a prayer meeting," Pauline laughed.

After the mornings chores were finished, I lit into my piano practice, banging out my frustrations with chords and scales. Near ten, the phone rang.

"Hi, this is Kathy Hansen. We met you Sunday in church, do you remember? My husband is Greg. We just started at the Bible college."

"Of course I remember you. How can I forget another Kathy from Washington? We love meeting people from our home state." Although we'd made time to warmly welcome the couple the Sunday before, I felt a bit puzzled by the call.

"Are you leaving for work?" Kathy asked.

"No, it's my day off, actually."

"Oh, good. Greg said he'd drive me over. I have something for you."

Ten minutes later, I opened the front door to a grinning couple.

"Surprise!" Kathy shoved a round, foil-wrapped container into my hands. "We received a box of apples from Washington this week. After meeting you on Sunday, I thought your family might like a little taste of home. Here's a fresh-baked apple pie."

My tears spilled onto the foil covering the still-warm pie.

"You are an apple pie angel," I thanked her between tears.

After I explained my unusual reaction to their gracious gift, tears glistened in her eyes. "Can you believe that a gift from our Washington friends could be used by God like that?"

Our family did eventually have the fried chicken dinner with mashed potatoes. But on Kathy Ann's sixteenth birthday, we ate our leftovers with a beautiful apple pie, the flaky crust crimped to perfection.

Twenty years have passed, and that pie is still a topic that comes up often in our family as we remember how God used my inadequate baking skills, a family gift from states away, and another Bible college family's encouraging spirit to give our daughter her heart's desire.

It was a gift directly from God—an apple pie baked and delivered by one of His angels. ☁

I KNOW HOW TO LIVE WHEN I AM POOR,
AND I KNOW HOW TO LIVE WHEN I HAVE PLENTY.
I HAVE LEARNED THE SECRET OF BEING HAPPY
AT ANY TIME IN EVERYTHING THAT HAPPENS,
WHEN I HAVE ENOUGH TO EAT AND
WHEN I GO HUNGRY, WHEN I HAVE MORE THAN I NEED
AND WHEN I DO NOT HAVE ENOUGH.
I CAN DO ALL THINGS THROUGH CHRIST,
BECAUSE HE GIVES ME STRENGTH.

PHILIPPIANS 4:12-13

They Said It

God never promises to remove us from our struggles.
He does promise, however, to change the way we look at them.

MAX LUCADO

Look at the bow in the cloud, in the very rain itself. That is a sign that
the sun, though you cannot see it, is shining still—that up above
beyond the cloud is still sunlight and warmth and cloudless blue sky.

CHARLES KINGSLEY

On days when life is difficult and I feel overwhelmed, as I do fairly
often, it helps to remember in my prayers that all God requires of
me is to trust Him and be His friend. I find I can do that.

BRUCE LARSON

You can't run away from trouble. There ain't no place that far.

UNCLE REMUS

Each of us may be sure that if God sends us on stony paths
He will provide us with strong shoes, and He will not send us
out on any journey for which He does not equip us well.

ALEXANDER MACLAREN

If you surrender to the wind, you can ride it.

TONI MORRISON

Troubles are often the tools by which God fashions us for better things.

HENRY WARD BEECHER

Who Loves the Rain

FRANCES SHAW

Who loves the rain
And loves his home,
And looks on life with quiet eyes,
Him will I follow through the storm;
And at his hearth-fire keep me warm;
Nor hell nor heaven shall that soul surprise,
Who loves the rain
And loves his home,
And looks on life with quiet eyes.

I'm not happy,
I'm cheerful.
There's a difference.
A happy woman has
no cares at all.
A cheerful woman has
cares but has learned
how to deal with them.

BEVERLY SILLS

It's All in the Attitude

BETTY KING

It all started when I was talking with a lady named Eileen at the library in McLeansboro, Illinois, about doing a book signing there. The library is housed in a beautiful old Victorian home, and if you have never toured the place, you should.

Anyway, we discussed the date and time I should be there, and before I hung up the phone, I asked about a handicapped-accessible entrance. Since I use a three-wheel scooter, I had a concern about its location.

"We don't have one," Eileen admitted flatly, "due to the age and restrictions on the building."

And just how am I going to get in the place? I thought, irritated. My attitude was nearing that stage where it needs a quick adjustment; I adjusted it and proceeded, speaking calmly.

"Well, how many steps are there? I might be able to use my walker or my canes," I said, thinking there were maybe one or two steps.

"Well, a few, but they have a good space between them," Eileen assured me.

After telling her that my husband and I would drive down and take her some posters and look at the steps, I hung up.

We went, we took, and we looked. Bill went in; I sat in the car. I was amazed at the beauty of the old home on the outside, including the finely aged, but fiercely daunting front staircase. What a wonderful place to have the town library—for able-bodied souls, that is!

Man, this is going to be some kind of a challenge, I thought, flabbergasted at the steps. I stared, thinking through possible ways to surmount the library entrance and wondering how in the world I was going to get in. There were more than one or two steps, mind you.

Later, over the phone, Eileen commented to me that someone assured her she could probably get someone from the nearby funeral home to assist me. Or perhaps the fire department would come to my rescue.

Sitting in my lift chair, with my scooter before me, I pictured six guys on either side of a pine box. A hook and ladder flashed in my mind's eye—the rescue squad.

Heaven help me! I was not liking this scenario. I was a cripple, mind you, but I was neither dead nor on fire.

Okay, Betty, calm down. Maybe you can find a story in all this, I was quick to think.

"Oh, the funeral home, huh? That should prove to be interesting," I said to her before hanging up the phone.

Well, the day came. Bill loaded the van with me, my scooter, my wheelchair, my canes and walker, and enough medical supplies to stock a small nursing home, and we headed for McLeansboro. (Bill really should have gotten a degree in nursing—or at least taken up football training.)

We arrived at the library, and there they were, waiting out front for me. I was expecting a big, black hearse and six guys standing lined up in front of the steps, or red lights flashing and sirens going off on a fire truck.

Instead there were two men, one of average build and the other a little smaller. Now, a junior ballerina I am not. I wondered what they had in mind.

"Are you from the funeral home?" I asked.

"Yes, I am," the larger of the two men answered.

"Well, I'm not real sure you two guys can handle this job! I'm not a featherweight, you know!"

After assuring me he was a paramedic with the funeral home and quite capable, I had no choice but to literally put my life in his hands (although I'm still trying to figure out what a paramedic does at a funeral home).

In no time at all, I was hoisted up the steps in my wheelchair. Where there's a will, there's a way, I guess.

I could have been embarrassed that I had to be hoisted up and down the stairs in front of God and everybody. But I chose not to let it darken my day. In fact, I chose to think of it as being ushered, like Cleopatra being carried along the Nile amid waving palm fronds.

I had my book signing and met some lovely people. I toured the library—well, the main floor, anyway—and oohed and aahed and browsed a little. The library directors answered my questions and were more than gracious to me. Then it was time to leave.

The owner of the funeral home himself appeared on the steps, and he brought his daughter along—apparently, the paramedic had something to attend to. The funeral director was a big guy; he looked like he could handle the situation. But her? Mercy me! What was she going to do? Let's all just go to the circus, why don't we!

I envisioned the sequence of events as they prepared to haul me out, a drum roll playing in my mind.

The funeral director managed to descend the steps with Bill on one side of my legs and the slightly-built man on the other. The funeral guy's daughter carried my purse. I guess that did take a little load off their backs; more junk was in my purse than just money and lipstick. After all, a girl has to be ready for whatever obstacles might come her way. Like a gargantuan staircase, for instance.

I could have been embarrassed that I had to be hoisted up and down the stairs in front of God and everybody. But I chose not to let it darken my day. In fact, I chose to think of it as being ushered, like Cleopatra being carried along the Nile amid waving palm fronds. Only there were no palm fronds—unless you count the weeds growing between the cracks in the parking lot.

It's all in the attitude. ☁

> WHEN YOU WALK, YOUR STEPS WILL NOT BE HINDERED,
> AND WHEN YOU RUN, YOU WILL NOT STUMBLE.
>
> **PROVERBS 4:12 NKJV**

Joke Break

The following jokes aren't terribly sophisticated. Okay, they're downright corny. But if these cheesy jokes help you hold onto your sanity for five more minutes, they've done their job.

What do you call a carpenter who loses his tools?
A saw loser.

How mad can a kangaroo get?
Hopping mad.

Why is the letter D so aggravating?
It makes Ma mad.

What's the kindest vegetable?
A sweet potato.

The Languages God Speaks

STAN MEEK

God speaks in dramatic ways:
In the swollen river's rage,
In the twister's path of terror, and
In the shudder and shake of the earthquake.

God speaks with quieter voice:
With the flutter of the butterfly's wings,
With the ceaseless changing of the cloud-studded sky,
With a cancer cell, a church bell,
And an empty tomb.

God speaks with soothing syllables,
The language of healing;
The soft answer and kind deed
In the face of wrath,
When the wounded whisper, "I forgive,"
And in all the selfless ways that give men room
And let them live.

God is a multi-linguist,
But His words are always couched
In the dialect of love.

LORD, EVERY MORNING YOU HEAR MY VOICE. EVERY MORNING,
I TELL YOU WHAT I NEED, AND I WAIT FOR YOUR ANSWER.

PSALM 5:3

Rain by the Numbers

- Nearly 80 inches of rain falls into the Amazon Basin each year. All that rain combines with over 1,000 tributary rivers to make the Amazon the highest-volume river in the world, contributing over 20% of all freshwater deposits in the world's oceans.

- Seattle reports only 58 clear days a year; Yuma, Arizona, reports 242.

- Most of the United States receives between 15 to 45 inches of rain annually.

- The world's one-minute rainfall record is held by Unionville, Maryland-the city received 1.23 inches of rain in one minute in July of 1956.

- Citrus farmers report that their crops require about 40 inches of rain a year.

Like it or not, into every life a little rain must fall. The good news is that God knows just how much rain will make us thrive—and provides a storm shelter for those unexpected cloudbursts.

*I will have nothing to do with
a God who cares only occasionally.
I need a God who is with us always,
everywhere, in the deepest depths
as well as the highest heights.
It is when things go wrong,
when good things do not happen,
when our prayers seem to have
been lost, that God is most present.
We do not need the sheltering
wings when things go smoothly.
We are closest to God in the
darkness, stumbling along blindly.*

MADELEINE L'ENGLE

Package Deal

DIANE DWYER AS TOLD TO CHRISTY PHILLIPPE

On that overcast October afternoon, I looked plenty pitiful. Standing at the barn beside my beat-up little travel trailer, with no car to pull it; my horse, with no trailer to transport him; and four trusting dogs, expecting me to feed them—I presented a sad sight. But we came as a package deal, and that day, there were no demands for package deals.

In the past I had asked God to lead me, and I tried to follow. But now doubts piled on top of one another. I had lost yet another job. Clearly, something was wrong. *Lord, have I chosen the wrong line of work?*

This time, I had been living in a three-bedroom, furnished mobile home on a large farm where I trained and cared for thirty horses and everything else that goes with that job. I love working with horses—have devoted forty-five years to it—but the work had gotten too hard for one person.

I dutifully wrote my employer a thirty-day notice of resignation. When I delivered the message, harsh words flew without warning, ending with my being told, "You are leaving now!"

Leaving! Where in the world will I go? I had counted on using those thirty days to train someone to take my place and to locate a new home for my "family." With my two sons grown and living away, that family now consisted of my horse and four dogs—almost as precious to me as my children.

My family stood there now, looking to me for answers: princely Swift Viking, my dark brown appendix quarter horse with the nickname of Vi-Guy; three basset hounds, a retired show dog named Lovey and two adoptees from the basset hound rescue named Lamar and Andrew; and Rudy, the precious miniature Dachshund I saved from almost certain euthanasia, having brought him home in a borrowed doggy wheelchair.

"Don't you worry, Vi-Guy," I said, stroking the white star on his forehead. "We'll find you a wonderful pasture, with a stream and a nice warm barn. Just you wait and see."

"And you guys," I said, kneeling down to hug the canine quartet demanding my attention. "We'll be OK. I know we will."

But inside, at that moment, I wondered if, when, and how I could fulfill those promises. "Lord," I cried out. "I need Your help here, real bad."

I phoned the teacher of my new Bible study class and shared my plight. "I'll be over in the morning to get your plants and care for them," she offered. "How else can I help?"

A few minutes later, a member of the class called. "Tomorrow I'll canvass stores in town for cardboard cartons to help you pack," she said.

Around 9:30 that night a young man who boarded his horse at the farm knocked on my door. His mother was with him. "We want to help you," she said. "You can park your trailer in our yard until you decide what to do."

The next morning, another boarder said, "I have an empty pasture. I'll keep Vi-Guy for you." Still another heard that conversation. "Vi-Guy will be lonely all by himself. I'll take my two donkeys out there to keep him company."

I couldn't believe the kindness of these people. Tears threatened to spill down my face when yet another boarder said, "Let me take your dogs to the kennel for a few days while you relocate. I'll pay the bill."

In spite of rain that lasted days, I managed to get my meager belongings into storage and prepare for the move. The hardest part was saying goodbye to Vi-Guy, knowing I couldn't see him often. Wearing a downcast face he leaned over, nudged me, and closed his eyes for my kiss.

Without my family, I was heartsick. Besides, my living conditions meant roughing it more than even I enjoy. It helped when I managed to get fencing up around the trailer so the dogs could come home. And things looked much better when another class member loaned me a car. Then I could get out and pound the turf, looking for work.

Through it all, every Sunday I attended the Bible study class and reported on my progress, or lack of it. The members encouraged me and prayed for me. And during those three months, I had many heart-to-heart talks with myself and with the Lord.

In one of our conversations I prayed, *Lord, You know how much I love horses and being outdoors. But if I'm supposed to be doing something else, please lead me to it.* Then I added, *But, Lord, if I'm in the right field, please let me know it without a shadow of a doubt.*

I've held "real" jobs, as my sons call them, but they just weren't me. Still, I thought I ought to give the other world one more try, so I applied for work at a local department store. The longer the interview took, the more uncomfortable I felt. *I can't do this!* I screamed inwardly. When the manager asked when I could start, I told him, "I'll have to let you know." I expressed my appreciation and hurried out into the sunshine.

Lord, thank You for that clear message. I know now that giving up the work I love is unthinkable.

Early one December morning, in my jacket pocket I felt a scrap of paper—that number I'd hesitated to call all these weeks. An inner voice said, *It's time to call it, Diane.* A lady named Vickie answered. "Why don't you come on over and talk with Brett?" she said.

"I'll be right there," I said, and by 8:30 I was turning into the entrance of picturesque Mountain Creek Ranch. I followed the gravel driveway as it curved around in front of the white frame main house to reveal a beautiful barn nestled in the middle of spectacular, rolling scenery.

A tour of the barn showed sixteen stalls (one of them empty), a bunkhouse, kitchen, shower facilities, even an office—all needing someone to use them. The answer to my prayers! My mind raced. Did I dare hope?

The answer to my prayers! My mind raced. Did I dare hope?

By noon my little trailer was snuggled against the side of that barn with a gorgeous view of wooded hills and mountain. Soon the fence was up and the dogs were exploring their new yard. And by evening, Vi-Guy was in the paddock meeting the other horses.

It's springtime now—a bright, warm afternoon. Birds sing their little hearts out, busy building nests. With their cheerful background music, I'm eating supper sitting beside my tiny trailer, now cozy as a cocoon. Nearby, Vi-Guy munches grass and the "boys" play at my feet.

Do I have any guarantees about tomorrow? No. But I'm confident that God knows and cares about my welfare. And that is enough.

So take another look. You'll see six happy campers: Vi-Guy, Lovey, Andrew, Lamar, Rudy—and me.

THE LORD IS GOOD TO THOSE WHO HOPE
IN HIM, TO THOSE WHO SEEK HIM.

LAMENTATIONS 3:25

Serve the Needy

One surefire way to bless yourself is to be a blessing to someone else. Volunteer for a day at a city mission or another favorite compassionate ministry. Or do something as simple as bake five or six dozen chocolate chip cookies and take a dozen each to your immediate neighbors.

*There is much in the
world to make us afraid.
There is much more
in our faith to
make us unafraid.*

FREDERICK W. CROPP

Fear in the Forest

NANCY MEANIX

The forest was so black I couldn't see my husband right next to me or my hand held up in front of my eyes. Something touched my leg. My stomach knotted, and I threw myself closer against Bob. We were both trembling, as much from fear as from the cold breeze coming down through the dense pines.

It was like being in a sealed closet—you know something solid is just beyond your nose and will soon surround and suffocate you.

How would we ever find our way out of the forest? How would we endure the frightening silence all night long? I kept remembering recent stories in our local paper about people stumbling upon black bears on forest trails, or sliding off slippery rocks into waterfalls. A bear had invaded our bird feeders just three weeks earlier.

Tourists had descended upon our town that June to admire the rhododendrons in the Pink Beds of Pisgah National Forest, ten miles from our mountain home in western North Carolina. We had yet to witness the beautiful flowers.

After a rainy day, the sun peeked out just before supper, so we ate quickly and left the dishes. We set out, dressed in golf shirts, thin shorts, and old sneakers, with light windbreakers tied around our waists.

We arrived at a sign at about 7:30: "Pink Beds Loop Trail." That meant, of course, a loop or circle that would return us right to our car—right?

Noting orange markings on that trail, we strolled onto it, holding hands as we had throughout our forty-three-year marriage. There were only a few "rhodies" along our level path, and we wanted to see more, perhaps around the next bend in the trail—or the next.

Much to our surprise, we came to an intersection in the trail. "I thought we were supposed to be on a loop," I wondered. Bob laughed, and we each tried to top the other's quips. Retired couple still missing after six weeks, we jokingly envisioned the headline.

We came to a large fallen tree, probably twenty inches around, and knew we had to stop and spend the whole night alone in the forest, without food or water, flashlight, matches, or sweaters.

On one wooden post hung two signs—"Pink Beds Loop Trail," said one, and "Beaver Dam. Trail Out," the other. So there was our answer: "Trail out," of course, meant "exit to parking lot."

The trail got narrower, wetter, finally becoming marsh and swamp. A sudden splash nearby made us realize we were by a large pond, and a beaver was broadcasting our invasion.

We had been walking for too long, and it was getting darker too quickly. I spotted a man-made bridge and hurried on, then slammed to a halt.

"The bridge is floating. It's not attached!" I shouted, my voice cracking, my eyes wet. "We can't get to it, or to the other side!"

So we turned around, and I faced the same numbing fear as we crossed those same slippery sites once more. At the "intersection," we decided to try the blue route instead of our orange one.

"It has to be closer. Let's try it," I sighed.

Now it was after 9:00. We walked faster, encouraging each other, but no longer joking. The path sloped upward and seemed unending. We considered finding a level dry place to take a nap or rest, then continue after our eyes adjusted. But all we found was rough terrain, fallen trees, gnarled roots, and prickly bushes grabbing at our bare legs.

We came to a large fallen tree, probably twenty inches around, and knew we had to stop and spend the whole night alone in the forest, without food or water, flashlight, matches, or sweaters.

By then, the night was so inky black that we knew where the other one was only by voice or crackling underfoot. We could not even make out each other's shape.

The stars so very high above us were our only companions throughout the night, except for fireflies. We were so glad to see them we began giving them names.

We did not sit or lie down all night because the ground was also muddy and cold. A strong wind made our windbreakers worthless, so we swung our arms, stamped our feet, and sang aloud a few favorite old songs.

But most often, and most importantly, we prayed. After a while, we began to reminisce about our many years together—about when Bob courted me in his Navy uniform while I worked in D.C.; about when Paul, one of our identical twin infants, succumbed to SIDS; about when our nine kids shared four bedrooms with endless noise and rivalries; about when they finally got married.

"What was that noise?" I hissed, poking at the blackness with a twisted branch.

"I think it's an owl. That owl will probably scare anything else away, and so will our prayers. Let's thank God for looking after us," Bob whispered in my ear.

So we began praying again. "Our Father, who art in heaven..." spilled from our lips in quivering tones. Then more hugs, hands locking around the other's neck. "Lead us not into temptation, but deliver us from evil...please, dear God," we continued.

As Bob kept up the family memories to keep me distracted, my mind started to panic as it again remembered that bear eating from our bird feeders.

Then I gave myself a lecture: *But you must stay strong and protect Bob's heart from too much strain.*

"What was that noise?" I hissed, poking at the blackness with a twisted branch.

We repeated the Lord's Prayer again and again as we recollected other traumas—when our grandson Tyler was born brain damaged; three years later when his baby cousin, Kelly, drowned in her backyard pool; when Bob suffered a heart attack at age forty-two and later underwent two bypass surgeries.

"We've pushed through so many crises together. We have no control over this situation now, honey," Bob whispered. "We must turn it over to God, and He will help us."

A few minutes later, a peace as palpable as the darkness filled the valley. I felt calm and safe. God had answered our vocal prayers and my silent one not to worry Bob. I realized that people really rise to the challenge in times of trauma with God's help. They get strength and courage, if they only ask.

I'm sure the night was just as black as it was before, but it suddenly seemed gray. I no longer dwelt on the terrifying possibility of bears or skunks or rabid raccoons behind the next tree. We kept praying, talking, singing, exercising, all the rest of that long night. We reaffirmed our love. We warmed and comforted each other.

Then, finally, the sky brightened and one bird broke the silence. We whistled back in joy. Little bushes sprang into focus. Now we could see Bob's watch—5:45!

The return trip of ninety minutes down the blue and then along the orange trail to the car seemed almost carefree by comparison. The sun was blazing and our mountains looked extraordinary.

We had been forest-people for twelve hours. We waved to everyone. They all looked so normal, so healthy, so rested, scurrying along just like any other day.

Our house warmly welcomed us from the road. We touched the grandchildren's pictures on the mantel. We threw our filthy clothes on the bathroom floor, showered off all that caked-on mud, and collapsed into bed. We were home, and we thanked God for it—out loud—before quickly falling asleep in each other's arms. ☁

YOU WON'T BE AFRAID OF SUDDEN TROUBLE;
YOU WON'T FEAR THE RUIN THAT COMES TO THE WICKED,
BECAUSE THE LORD WILL KEEP YOU SAFE.
HE WILL KEEP YOU FROM BEING TRAPPED.

PROVERBS 3:25–26

Last Lines

EMILY BRONTE

No coward soul is mine,
No trembler in the world's storm-troubled sphere:
I see Heaven's glories shine,
And faith shines equal, arming me from fear.

O God within my breast,
Almighty, ever-present Deity!
Life—that in me has rest,
As I—undying Life—have power in Thee!

Vain are the thousand creeds
That move men's hearts: unutterably vain;
Worthless as withered weeds,
Or idlest froth amid the boundless main,

To waken doubt in one
Holding so fast by Thine infinity;
So surely anchored on
The steadfast rock of immortality.

With wide-embracing love
Thy Spirit animates eternal years,
Pervades and broods above,
Changes, sustains, dissolves, creates, and rears.

Though earth and man were gone,
And suns and universes cease to be,
And Thou were left alone,
Every existence would exist in Thee.

There is not room for Death,
Nor atom that his might could render void:
Thou—Thou art Being and Breath,
And what Thou art may never be destroyed.

I TRUST IN YOUR LOVE.
MY HEART IS HAPPY
BECAUSE YOU SAVED ME.

PSALM 13:5

The Cloudburst

MELINDA LANCASTER

Several years ago, my husband and I took a trip to Hawaii to celebrate our wedding anniversary. Not wanting to waste any precious fun time trying to navigate the unfamiliar paradise of Oahu, we decided to sign up for a tour package.

One afternoon, our group boarded the bus to go to one of the national parks. Since this was a romantic getaway for us, I had taken great pains to look beautiful for the tour. With every hair in place, my outfit neatly ironed, I got on the bus with a vision in my mind of "making a memory" together that would be frozen in time.

We arrived at the park and immediately we could see that it was unlike any other we had ever seen. Strolling along, holding hands, we set out on our romantic adventure. The sun was shining, and with the dewy breeze lightly blowing, it was almost like being in paradise. That is, until a wayward raindrop hit me on the head.

Before I could even look up to see where it came from, we were in the middle of a cloudburst that left us both soaking wet.

My husband still looked fine to me—love is blind (or so they say). I, on the other hand, was certain that I looked just like I felt—like a drowned rat. The tears rolled down my cheeks in perfect timing with the raindrops. We were making a memory, all right, but in this memory I was not the island goddess I had planned to be. My hair was plastered to my head like a kewpie doll. I was soaked through and completely miserable. But my spirit and enthusiasm were even more dampened than my clothing.

Greg, being the fine husband he is, did his best to comfort me. Here we were in a beautiful park with banana and coconut trees, soothing Hawaiian music playing, and many sights yet to see—he was not about to let the storm rain on our parade. I, being the resilient, levelheaded sort of woman who can cope with unexpected changes, just wanted to go back to the hotel room.

Fortunately, that was impossible. As we continued walking through the park, the rain stopped, and that warm tropical breeze began to quickly dry out our clothing. As for my hair—well, that was unrecoverable.

In the distance, we saw a beautiful waterfall. As we approached it, there were cliff divers that looked like tiny specks standing at the top. They took turns diving—soaring over what seemed like thousands of feet to me—striking graceful, beautiful poses. Even more memorable was the vivid rainbow that began to form over the top of the waterfall. It looked painted personally, just for us, by the hand of God. I sighed contentedly, took Greg's hand, and forgot all about my hair. ☁

If you spend your whole life waiting for the storm,
you'll never enjoy the sunshine.

MORRIS WEST

Talk About Bad Weather

1 KINGS 18:21-39

The fact that there's a cable channel dedicated exclusively to weather doesn't mean we are the first generation to keep a constant watch on what's happening outside. In fact, throughout human history, particularly in light of the onetime dominance of an agrarian society, the weather has been a huge topic of discussion, from Socrates and other ancients to Poor Richard's Almanac and your nightly news.

The biggest worry in biblical times wasn't the threat of too much rain and flooding—that story about Noah notwithstanding—but of the opposite condition: drought.

In 1 Kings 18, we discover that the nation of Israel went more than three years without rain. Talk about bad weather. Crop failure and famine were rampant. One prophet of God, Elijah, took this opportunity to reveal to the people that they, following King Ahab, had turned away from the One True God: "He did more things to make the Lord, the God of Israel, angry than all the other kings before him" (1 Kings 16:33). He would pray for rain on their behalf, but it was time for them to turn back to God and be faithful to Him: "How long will you not decide between two choices? If the Lord is the true God, follow him, but if Baal is the true God, follow him!" (1 Kings 18:21).

Jesus points out that rain falls on both the righteous and the unrighteous. So when we are surprised by problems and challenges, we need not assume God is punishing us to by sending calamities our way.

But hardship and trials are fires of refinement, where we can grow in character and faith. As James told early followers of Jesus who were facing persecution: "When you have many kinds of troubles, you should be full of joy" (1:2)

We might not always be able to find the joy in flooding or droughts, but we can experience the remarkable peace of God, which "surpasses all understanding" (Philippians 4:7 NKJV). ☁

> DON'T WORRY ABOUT ANYTHING;
> INSTEAD, PRAY ABOUT EVERYTHING.
> TELL GOD WHAT YOU NEED,
> AND THANK HIM FOR ALL HE HAS DONE.
>
> **PHILIPPIANS 4:6 NLT**

God's Promises for the Unexpected

God will...

Never leave you
God has said, "I will never leave you;
I will never forget you."
HEBREWS 13:5

Never stop loving you
The Lord's love never ends;
his mercies never stop.
LAMENTATIONS 3:22

Give you joy as you trust Him
We rejoice in him, because we trust his holy name.
PSALM 33:21

Be a refuge in times of trouble
God is our protection and our strength.
He always helps in times of trouble.
PSALM 46:1

Give you security
Those who trust the Lord are like Mount Zion,
which sits unmoved forever.

PSALM 125:1

Give you hope for the future
"I know what I am planning for you," says the Lord.
"I have good plans for you, not plans to hurt you.
I will give you hope and a good future."

JEREMIAH 29:11

Guard your heart in times of trouble
And God's peace, which is so great
we cannot understand it, will keep your
hearts and minds in Christ Jesus.

PHILIPPIANS 4:7

Be with you
The Lord your God fights for you,
as he promised to do.

JOSHUA 23:10

A Prayer of Hope and Gratitude

Dear Heavenly Father,

I know that no matter how hard I try, I can't control everything in my life. Lord, please remind me of Your great strength and great compassion today. Give me the faith of Hannah and David and Abraham, who trusted and depended on You in the midst of the difficulties they faced.

Thank You that You hear me when I call to You—You listen and have infinite patience and care to hear my thoughts as I bring my needs and praise before You.

THUNDERSTORMS

The acid test of our faith in the promises of God is never found in the easygoing, comfortable ways of life, but in the great emergencies, the times of storm and of stress, the days of adversity, when all human aid fails.

ETHEL BELL

Did you hear that thunder clap? That sounded close. The kids should be running downstairs and jumping in bed any second now. Can't remember if I powered down the computer, but should probably check. This is one of those nights when you could lose a hard drive.

Wow! That one was even closer. If the kids don't hurry down here, I might have to run upstairs.

Ben Franklin may have been filled with practical wisdom, but someone needed to tell him it ain't smart to flight a kite in an electrical storm.

Some rainy days are gentle and soothing, but some are raging and dangerous and set our nerves on edge.

Sometimes life is like that, too. When the storms grow fierce, all we can do is cry out to Jesus for help, just like Peter. As you peruse these next pages, find comfort in the story of Jesus calming the storm, and inspiration in "The Heart of an Angel." May you find the courage you need to face the storms in your life today.

THE LORD GOD IS MY STRENGTH.
HE MAKES ME LIKE A DEER THAT DOES NOT
STUMBLE SO I CAN WALK ON THE STEEP MOUNTAINS.

HABAKKUK 3:19

It's a good thing to have all the props pulled out from under us occasionally. It gives us some sense of what is rock under our feet, and what is sand.

MADELEINE L'ENGLE

God Calms the Storms of Our Lives

NANCY B. GIBBS

Life is not easy. Most of us can attest to that fact. When creditors threaten, when doctors warn, when rivers of tears flow down our cheeks, we realize how difficult life can sometimes be.

At these times, we have two choices: We can buckle under the turmoil, or we can look to God above. We can decide that we cannot and will not take another step, or we can ride on God's mighty shoulders.

As God's children, He has promised to carry us regardless of the choices we make. We can be happy, praise, and rejoice in God's faithfulness, or we can whine, complain, and cry as we struggle along. Personally, I have found that my heart can sing regardless of the storms around me, as long as I allow Jesus to live inside me. When I try to follow His will for my life, Jesus is faithful to show me the way.

My life sometimes becomes chaotic, just like everyone else's. There is oftentimes too much month at the end of the money. At times, I become disappointed when things don't go as I would like. And I have to confess that my heart has been broken a time a two over the years. During some of the bleakest times of my life, however, I have also learned some valuable lessons.

I have learned to stand firm in the midst of the storms, knowing that God wants to control every storm I encounter. During the raging storms, I must rely fully on God by surrendering myself to Him. As soon as I think I have control of certain areas of my life, I find that my grip loosens.

How could I comfort a grieving soul if I never grieved myself? How could I understand how an ailing person feels, had I never experienced problems with my health? How could I relate to those who are sin-sick, if I had never found myself begging God to forgive me?

I discover my humanness, and I have found that life as a human being isn't painless. Our emotions sometimes cause us to stumble and fall. God can pick us up when we find that we can no longer stand on our own.

I have learned that during trials, my strength is magnified. If I never had to face adversity, I would never fully appreciate the calm, joyful times that come my way. The times when God has strengthened my faith most greatly were the times I completely surrendered my cares and concerns to Him.

I have also learned that it is through my own difficulties that I have been able to minister to other people. How could I comfort a grieving soul if I never grieved myself? How could I understand how an ailing person feels, had I never experienced problems with my health? How could I relate to those who are sin-sick, if I had never found myself begging God to forgive me?

Even with Jesus on the boat with them, the disciples panicked in the face of a storm. With only three words, "Quiet! Be still," Jesus calmed the storm, causing the wind to die down and the water to become calm. Isn't this proof to us today that God's power remains with us when we trust and call on Him?

There is no storm greater than God's power. There is no greater love than that of our Savior, Jesus. When the storms in life seem too big for us to handle, let us remember that God wants to manage them for us. ☁

I LEAVE YOU PEACE;
MY PEACE I GIVE YOU.
I DO NOT GIVE IT TO YOU
AS THE WORLD DOES.
SO DON'T LET YOUR HEARTS
BE TROUBLED OR AFRAID.

JOHN 14:27

They Said It

Snuggle in God's arms.
When you are hurting, when you feel lonely, left out, let Him cradle
you, comfort you, reassure you of His all-sufficient power and love.

KAY ARTHUR

Prosperity is a great teacher; adversity is a greater.

WILLIAM HAZLITT

Every problem has in it the seeds of its own solution.
If you don't have any problems, you don't get any seeds.

NORMAN VINCENT PEALE

You may not realize it when it happens,
but a kick in the teeth may be the best thing in the world for you.

WALT DISNEY

When God is involved, anything can happen. Be open. Stay that way.
God has a beautiful way of bringing good vibrations out of broken
chords.

CHUCK SWINDOLL

I know God will not give me anything I can't handle.
I just wish He didn't trust me so much.

MOTHER TERESA

He restores my soul;
He leads me in the paths
of righteousness
For His name's sake.

PSALM 23:3 NKJV

The soul would have no rainbow had the eyes no tears.

JOHN VANCE CHENEY

The Heart of an Angel

SHERI PLUCKER

The phone rang. We were waiting for a call, and with a deep breath I picked up the receiver. Our doctor revealed the results of my amniocentesis.

"Your test was positive for Trisomy 21," he said softly.

My hand began quivering. Then there was silence, and I dropped the phone.

I sat down on the stairs, wondering, Why is this happening to us? Our two sons were horrified by my cries and quickly ran up the stairs to hug me. I'll never forget the comfort they gave. We sat on the stairs clinging to one another as I cried.

My dad walked in moments later, and I ran to him with the news. He held me in his arms and, though I could see the pain in his eyes, said, "God will take care of you." We knew only God could help heal this pain. There wasn't a moment when tears weren't streaming down my cheeks long into the night.

After months of anticipation, our daughter Hailey was born. Shortly after coming home from the hospital, I struggled to feed her three ounces of formula in an hour. After a series of tests and a continued decline in appetite, she underwent her first open-heart surgery at only three and a half months old. At first her eating improved, but gradually it became apparent that the surgery was unsuccessful. God continued to challenge us to accept these difficult times and trust in Him.

We scheduled her second surgery for March at a children's hospital in Seattle. Hailey was only nine months old and weighed thirteen pounds. We knew her life was at risk as we waited for the surgical team to arrive. I squeezed Hailey close and touched my lips to her cheek as tears pooled in my eyes. I pleaded with God, "Please protect our little girl."

I glanced down at my wide-eyed daughter, who appeared to be thinking, *Why all the fuss?* Little did she know the events that were about to happen.

After months of anticipation, our daughter Hailey was born. Shortly after coming home from the hospital, I struggled to feed her three ounces of formula in an hour. After a series of tests and a continued decline in appetite, she underwent her first open-heart surgery at only three and a half months old.

Moments later, two members of the surgical team whisked open the curtain. The anesthesiologist said, "We're ready for Hailey."

I prayed for her safety as I pressed Hailey close to my chest. Tears clouded my vision as the anesthesiologist lifted her from my arms and faded in the distance.

I mumbled between sobs, "I'll see you soon," my heart melting. Then, once again, the Lord reminded me that Hailey's life was in His hands. My part was to trust in Him.

Three hours and thirty-four minutes later, the surgeon stepped off the elevator and said, "Hailey's surgery was successful!" This time there were tears of joy.

Later, I walked into the intensive care unit as my eyes glanced over her listless and fragile body. A blanket of countless wires and cords ran across her body, connecting her to an array of high-tech machines. I walked towards my helpless daughter's bedside, overwhelmed. My fingers touched Hailey's limp hand, and I assured her of my presence with a whisper: "I love you, Hailey. Mommy is right here next to you."

As Hailey recovered, each day brought an inner strength in Hailey we had never seen before. After six days, we were released from the hospital with a healthy daughter prepared to take on the world with her spunky personality.

My dad's words were true—God will take care of us. God has drawn us and many others closer to Him through the smile and grace of a little girl with Down syndrome. He has taught us to accept one another for who we are and to trust in Him during the challenges of life.

Hailey is now five years old and continues to keep us on our toes. Early each morning, she climbs out of bed, sneaks downstairs, and yells, "Surprise! Hailey help you." Instantly, my heart skips a beat and I stop the treadmill. I step off, squeeze her tight, and our morning ritual begins—running around the house in a game of chase.

Hailey is now five years old and continues to keep us on our toes.

We visit the cardiologist every six months for an update on Hailey's heart. They continue to monitor her leaky mitral valve and have recently added a new medicine. Daily, I pray for God to protect Hailey's heart as I trust in Him.

Many times a day, we give thanks for the special gift that was delivered to our family for a reason: To touch the lives of others with her captivating laughter and love. Truly, I believe, Hailey has the heart of an angel.

IN THEIR MISERY THEY CRIED OUT TO THE LORD,
AND HE SAVED THEM FROM THEIR TROUBLES.
HE STILLED THE STORM AND CALMED THE WAVES.

PSALM 107:28-29

With Skin On

CHRISTY PHILLIPPE

Mark's wife attended a weekly Bible study, and so each Monday night, it was his turn to stay home with their four-year-old son, Justin.

The schedule was usually set: Right after Mom left, Mark and Justin would have their customary tickle-fest, and then Mark would make sure Justin had his supper and a bath. Then it was story time, after which Mark would kiss Justin's head, tuck him into bed, and head downstairs to watch his favorite TV show at 9 P.M.

But one particular Monday night, the hero of the show was just about to save the day—when a terrible thunderstorm blew in, with lightning and loud, booming thunder.

"Dad, I'm scared!" Justin shouted. "Come up here with me!"

"Oh, no," Mark mumbled, reluctant to miss the end of the show. "Don't worry, Justin," he called out. "You'll be all right. You know God loves you."

"I do know God loves me," cried Justin, "but I need someone with skin on."

Joke Break

The trials and storms of life are nothing to make light of—or are they? While these jokes may not have you laughing out loud or even chuckling, they might just drown out the thunder in your stormy day.

What does the voice of experience say?
Ouch.

What do tailors do when they get tired?
They just press on.

What did the dust say to the rain?
If this keeps up, my name will be Mud.

*The best way out of a
problem is through it.*

AUTHOR UNKNOWN

The River

MAX DAVIS

I am an outdoor enthusiast. On any given Saturday you can find me hiking through the woods. A while back I was hiking along some rocky cliffs that had a cool river running between them. A bridge crossed the river, but the cliffs and the bridge ran together so it appeared there was no way to get down to the river. The cliffs were not that high—maybe thirty feet, but they were steep and unclimbable without any gear. My heart was set on the river, though, and I was determined to get down there.

So I slid down as far as I could, and then I jumped. It was crazy, I know. I just made a calculated risk and jumped. After scouting the situation, I was certain that the place I would land would be safe. Plus, I was taught how to land and roll safely in a rappelling course. I viewed it as a challenge.

The jump was a success. As soon as my feet hit the ground, though, a thought hit me. How was I going to get back up? Getting down was the easy part. Getting back up was going to take a miracle.

But I was down there, so I decided to enjoy the river for a while. I played in the river for about an hour and realized I had better start heading back and figure out how to get back up. As I walked and thought about it, the more I realized the seriousness of my situation. I started to get scared. I prayed a simple prayer to God: *Lord, help me.*

Then an amazing thing happened. I looked down, and I'm telling the truth, there was a long nylon rope just lying there. In the middle of nowhere. It was just lying there as if someone knew I was going to need it. I couldn't believe it! Obviously an ordinary hiker had left it there who knows how long ago, but I saw it as a miracle.

As I approached the bridge, I started calculating how to best utilize the rope. Then another thought hit me. Yes, I had a rope. Yes, I had a way out—but I wasn't out yet, and it wasn't going to be easy.

For what seemed like an eternity, I tried to find a way to throw the rope so it would catch on the bridge or a rock or something so I could pull myself up. Finally I found a little crack in the wall of the bridge, about an inch wide. I tied a knot on the rope, and after a lot of tries, the rope slid in the crack. Thankfully, the knot held it there. Relief. But I still had to climb the rope.

Because I was climbing up the bridge, I had nowhere to put my feet for leverage. The rope was just hanging down in the air. Have you ever tried to climb a twenty-foot rope in midair? It's not easy. It took all the strength I had just to make it to the top of the bridge. When I finally made it up, my shouts of jubilation echoed throughout the canyon.

While pondering the incident, I saw some striking parallels between it and our personal lives. Before I could get out of the canyon, first I had to admit that I had made a huge error in judgment. Then I had to take some steps to change the situation. One step was prayer. God provided a rope. But then I had to do my part. And it was hard work. God did not send an angel to lift me out of the canyon. He did not climb the rope for me. What He did was provide a way out, but it was up to me to utilize His provision.

The same pattern holds in our personal lives. God often gives us just enough rope to climb out of the dark holes we are experiencing. Yet if we don't take personal responsibility in practical areas and work hard, we won't get anywhere.

TRUST IN THE LORD WITH ALL YOUR HEART;
DO NOT DEPEND ON YOUR OWN UNDERSTANDING.
SEEK HIS WILL IN ALL YOU DO,
AND HE WILL DIRECT YOUR PATHS.

PROVERBS 3:5-6 NLT

*Just as there comes
a warm sunbeam into
every cottage window,
so comes a love born
of God's care for
every separate need.*

NATHANIEL HAWTHORNE

A Ray of Sunshine

CINDY L. HEFLIN

I sat in silence by the kitchen window, watching autumn leaves tumble in the early morning drizzle. The damp, dreary scene outside seemed to mirror my discouraged spirit. Sipping a steaming cup of tea, I scanned the overcast skies for the slightest glimpse of sunlight. While my children slept, I lingered alone, deep in thought. Though longing to feel the warmth of God's presence, my hot cup of tea did little to change the climate of my numb heart. I whispered a faint prayer, asking God for help and a ray of sunshine to pierce the clouds of my despair.

Always independent and self-sufficient, I felt uncomfortable asking for help, unwilling to burden others. The challenge of my new limitations overwhelmed me.

Several weeks had passed since the car accident and the ophthalmology report that slammed the brakes on my independence. My doctor's painful announcement still echoed in my mind—"...vision severely deteriorated ...irreversible damage...never drive again..." It crushed me to face my visual limitations and the certainty of gradual blindness.

Suddenly, the children's playful voices suspended my thoughts, signaling the start of another busy day. I muddled through a typical morning of breakfast, laundry, and play dough, struggling to understand why God allowed this to happen. Though overcome with despair, I knew He would take care of our needs—but how?

My husband frequently traveled out-of-state on business—for days, sometimes weeks, at a time. With two young daughters to care for, my days were busy with trips to the supermarket, preschool, and pediatrician. Always independent and self-sufficient, I felt uncomfortable asking for help, unwilling to burden others. The challenge of my new limitations overwhelmed me. Even with God's help, it seemed impossible to cope with this sudden change in my life.

> I realized traveling with Mary was more than just a trip to the bank, drugstore, or post office—it was fun.

Weary from a long afternoon and a heavy heart, I collapsed on the sofa as the telephone rang. To my surprise, the friendly caller was Mary, a young mom from our church. Despite our mutual friends, we had never met, but she compassionately expressed her concern for me and my family. Gently, she offered, "You know, I'm always out with my two children. I'd really love the company if you ever need a ride." A tear slipped down my cheek as we made plans to run errands together one day each week.

I hung up the phone, my heart overflowing with amazement and gratitude. God had heard my feeble prayer and faithfully answered.

After baths and bedtime stories, I kissed my girls goodnight with a new sense of peace in my spirit and a tiny seed of hope growing in my heart. Blissfully exhausted, I fell into bed, thanking the Lord for His provision.

Mary arrived promptly the next afternoon. Her bright smile and cheerful nature were as sunny as her buttercup-colored sedan. Each Tuesday at noon, with the children buckled securely and the car stocked with plenty of books and snacks, we set out for an afternoon on the road. Soon, I realized traveling with Mary was more than just a trip to the bank, drugstore, or post office—it was fun. With games and songs, she entertained the children as we made our rounds "all through the town." Her joy and laughter were good medicine to my weary soul.

A day with optimistic Mary included lively conversation that always lifted my spirits. Discussions often centered on our faith in Christ as she encouraged me to seek Him for the strength to overcome my trials. On difficult days, she reminded me that all things are possible with God.

Before long, icy winds whistled in the barren branches spanning the gray winter sky. Housebound against my will, I often felt shrouded in isolation like a tulip bulb trapped beneath the frozen ground. But a snowy afternoon spent at Mary's warm and welcoming home always cured my cabin fever. Her gift of hospitality was as comforting as a blazing hearth at a charming country inn.

Over a cup of hot chocolate, we talked and laughed while the little ones napped and the preschoolers played Candyland on the floor nearby. Soft brown curls framed the sparkling blue eyes and contagious smile that reflected Mary's radiant personality. "In seasons of joy or pain, always remember—God's love for you is greater than you can ever imagine," she said. "We're all someone special in His eyes!"

The truth of her simple words of encouragement shot straight into my heart, compelling me to keep trusting the Lord.

Soon the scent of apple blossoms filled the air and the welcome spring sunshine lit a new hope in my spirit. In addition to our weekly trek, Mary often invited my kids and me to the playground, a picnic in the park, or "Mommy and Me" day at the YMCA. Enjoying these simple pleasures with my daughters once again meant so much to me.

My despair diminished and my faith grew stronger as I learned to focus on the Lord's faithfulness and compassion: During my darkest days, He sent a cherished friend to lighten my burdens and bless me in so many ways.

God had faithfully provided for my needs—and more than I dared to ask or imagine. Seeing the generosity and encouragement of Mary and other caring friends and family, I am daily motivated to follow their example. For I know that sharing God's hope with others is like a ray of sunshine on a cloudy day. ☁

EVERY GOOD ACTION AND EVERY PERFECT GIFT IS FROM GOD.
THESE GOOD GIFTS COME DOWN FROM THE CREATOR OF
THE SUN, MOON, AND STARS, WHO DOES NOT CHANGE
LIKE THEIR SHIFTING SHADOWS.

JAMES 1:17

Rhyme It

When was the last time you sat down to compose a poem? Your senior year of high school? A project in a creative writing course? Let your creativity and spirit soar over the next hour or two as you express what is in your heart in rhyme and meter.

God Will Keep You Safe

ACTS 27

Sometimes we get inklings that stormy weather is ahead, but Paul absolutely knew what awaited him and his captors if they set sail from Crete. He warned: "Men, I can see there will be a lot of trouble on this trip. The ship, the cargo, and even our lives may be lost" (Acts 27:10).

It's true the harbor in Crete was not ideal for wintering, but it was winter nonetheless, not the season to set sail on the Mediterranean. The centurion in charge of Paul, already impatient with delays, took a soft southern wind as a sign that fortune was on their side.

But only a few days later on open water, a gale-force "northeaster," a strong storm very familiar to those who live in the New England states, hit them head-on.

They shipwrecked on the island of Malta, where Paul spoke a classic "I told you so": "Men, you should have listened to me. You should not have sailed from Crete. Then you would not have all this trouble and loss" (Acts 27:21).

If anyone understood storms and hardships, it was Paul—

- He was attacked by a mob who didn't like his teaching and left for dead (Acts 21:30-32).
- He was imprisoned for being a Christian (Acts 16:23).
- He was criticized by church people who liked other leaders better (2 Corinthians 10:10, 12:11).
- He even had physical problems (Galatians 4:13).

Yet, this is the same man who could boldly tell this group: "None of you will lose even one hair off your heads" (Acts 27:34), and the man who could declare to others—

"But in all these things we have full victory through God who showed his love for us. Yes, I am sure that neither death, nor life, nor angels, nor ruling spirits, nothing now, nothing in the future, no powers, nothing above us, nothing below us, nor anything else in the whole world will ever be able to separate us from the love of God that is in Christ Jesus our Lord" (Romans 8:37-39).

No matter what storms are shaking your life and faith today, rest assured that God's love is greater and stronger than anything you're facing.

Faith is not a storm cellar to which men and women can flee for refuge from the storms of life. It is, instead, an inner force that gives them the strength to face those storms and their consequences with serenity of spirit.

SAM J. ERVIN, JR.

God's Promises in the Midst of Storms

God will...

Walk with you through troubled times

When you pass through the waters, I will be with you.
When you cross rivers, you will not drown.
When you walk through fire, you will not be burned,
nor will the flames hurt you.

ISAIAH 43:2

Enable you to conquer your life's storms

The Lord God is my strength. He makes me like a deer that
does not stumble so I can walk on the steep mountains.

HABAKKUK 3:19

Hear your prayers

The Lord our God comes near when we pray to him.

DEUTERONOMY 4:7

Protect you
The angel of the Lord camps around those
who fear God, and he saves them.

PSALM 34:7

Stay close to you
Even if I walk through a very dark valley,
I will not be afraid, because you are with me.
Your rod and your walking stick comfort me.

PSALM 23:4

Care for you
Give all your worries to him, because he cares about you.

1 PETER 5:7

Give you grace
Let us, then, feel very sure that we can come
before God's throne where there is grace.
There we can receive mercy and grace
to help us when we need it.

HEBREWS 4:16

A Prayer for Help and Courage

Dear Heavenly Father,

My life doesn't feel very stable right now.
Lord, You know the things I'm facing. I need
Your counsel today. I need Your strength and peace.
Lord, I pray that You would come beside me
and help me remember that You're there.

Thank You for Your goodness. Thank You
that Your love and grace are enough to see me
through the darkest of times.

BLUE DAYS

Some days you're a bug,
some days you're a windshield.

PRICE COBB

Sigh. Should really get moving and get something done. Okay, I really am going to get up and shake a leg in five more minutes. Sigh.

I ought to jog around the neighborhood or do some crunches or both. They say that exercise helps clear the cobwebs from the mind and spirit. Sigh.

Okay, just five more minutes...

Sometimes rainy-day blues have nothing to do with the weather. The summer sun may be shining brightly, the fall season may be particularly crisp and colorful, your winter day may be brisk outside but warm and cheery by the fireplace, or your spring afternoon may be filled with gentle showers and brilliant flowers—but you still feel down and blue.

The poet St. John of the Cross talked about the "dark night of the soul," and sometimes that's just what the blues feel like. Maybe you can't make yourself feel cheery, but there are resources available—friends, prayer, and, yes, exercise—to help you find your way while you walk toward a fresh new day.

BUT EVEN THE DARKNESS IS NOT DARK TO YOU.
THE NIGHT IS AS LIGHT AS THE DAY; DARKNESS
AND LIGHT ARE THE SAME TO YOU.

PSALM 139:12

*Never forget to look for
blessings—even the smallest
of joys can brighten
the worst of days.*

ANONYMOUS

See You at Home

MELANIE BACHMAN

"You have got to be kidding me." In the gray pre-dawn glow, I could see my dog, Snuffy, sitting on the floor, looking at me. Each morning, she hopped off the bed, giving me my cue to get up and let her out. Surely it wasn't time yet. Surely she had woken up early and would understandingly allow me ten more minutes. I blearily made out the numbers on our clock. Much to my dismay, Snuffy was running right on schedule.

My husband, John, grasped for his glasses and said something like, "Mfffrgh." I reached over and pushed them into his hand.

We were a little glum over breakfast. The news droned from the small TV in the kitchen. Cloudy all day. Don't take the expressway south of 45th. Our alma mater lost.

John spoke first. "What do you have going on today?"

"I don't know. Staff meeting. Kathy and I really need to start getting ready for next week's conference. All that stuff. You?"

"The usual," he replied with his mouth full.

Before we knew it, it was 7:09, officially time to hurry. After a flurry of showers and toothbrushes and "Have you seen a shoe that looks just like this one?" I poured some coffee into a travel mug, then set about collecting my lunch and shoulder bag.

Seven minutes later, I had just gotten on the highway and started to reach for my coffee, then cursed my forgetfulness when I realized it was still sitting on the kitchen counter.

My cell phone rang. It was John. "Hi," I said.

"Hey, is this coffee for me? That's so nice."

"Um, no. I kind of poured that for me. But I guess you can have it."

THE RAINY DAY BOOK

"Aww, how sweet. I love you, snoogie-woogie," he said, imitating that syrupy tone we had so often mocked in other couples.

"Don't mention it," I groaned, hoping he could hear me smile.

The rest of the day plodded on. There was extra traffic on the highway, extra paperwork on my desk, extra spam in my inbox. I hoped an extra cup of coffee at lunch would make up for the cup I'd lost that morning. But it didn't, and to make matters worse, I ended up staying an extra thirty minutes.

I came home, threw my bag on the floor, kicked off my heels, and wondered what on earth I was going to make for dinner. I shook Snuffy's furry brown ears. "Have you been out? Where's Daddy?"

> The rest of the day plodded on. There was extra traffic on the highway, extra paperwork on my desk, extra spam in my inbox.

I could hear John in the kitchen. When I walked in, the first thing I saw was our kitchen table, laden with Styrofoam boxes with a familiar logo on them. Then I saw John, sorting through a plastic takeout bag and trying to look casual.

"You went to Chan's."

"Yes, I did."

"That's my favorite place."

"Um, yeah, I actually already knew that. That was sort of the point?"

Snuffy scampered out of the way as I squeezed him by the elbows and smiled at him. "Thank you, snoogie-woogie." ☁

Spring Cleaning

No need to add guilt to discouragement, so don't take this suggestion too far. But why don't you identify one area of your house—even the kitchen drawer with coupons and bills stuffed in it—and do some cleaning and organizing? You'll feel better!

Tune In

Studies show that music diminishes the physiological effects of stress, including heart rate, blood pressure, and cortisol levels. Music can make you happy—it can evoke emotions, revive memories, and according to some researchers, may stimulate the same areas in the brain as food, sex, and drugs.

Whether it's slow, soothing strains to sympathize with our sadness or perky beats to shake us out of a rut, the right formula of music is sometimes just what the doctor ordered. So hop on your favorite (legal) download site or pull your favorite CDs off the shelf and make yourself a feel-better mix tape.

Here are a few soul-soothing starters:

- "Shoot the Moon" by Norah Jones
- Schubert's Ave Maria
- "No Regrets" by Jennifer Knapp
- "Why Georgia" by John Mayer
- "Small Enough" by Nichole Nordeman
- "Here With Me" by Mercy Me
- "This Side" by Nickel Creek
- "When Love Takes You In" by Steven Curtis Chapman
- "All that I Am" by the Afters
- "On Fire" by Switchfoot

They Said It

Sadness is almost never anything but a form of fatigue.

ANDRE GIDE

Every Christian has a very personal responsibility to grow in their faith. Yet there are times when we seem to stand still. That is when God touches us like the earth in the springtime, bringing new growth and warmth for the faithful souls dedicated to His service.

ED PRICE

Whether life is good or bad, God's goodness, rooted in His character, is the same.

HELEN GRACE LESCHEID

Sadness is but a wall between two gardens.

KAHLIL GIBRAN

I've got dreams in hidden places and extra smiles for when I'm blue.

AUTHOR UNKNOWN

Even in the winter, even in the midst of the storm, the sun is still there. Somewhere, up above the clouds, it still shines and warms and pulls at the life buried deep inside the brown branches and frozen earth. The sun is there! Spring will come! The clouds cannot stay forever.

GLORIA GAITHER

The Rainy Day

HENRY WADSWORTH LONGFELLOW

The day is cold, and dark, and dreary;
It rains, and the wind is never weary;
The vine still clings to the moldering wall,
But at every gust the dead leaves fall,
And the day is dark and dreary.

My life is cold, and dark, and dreary;
It rains, and the wind is never weary;
My thoughts still cling to the moldering Past,
But the hopes of youth fall thick in the blast
And the days are dark and dreary.

Be still, sad heart! and cease repining;
Behind the clouds is the sun still shining;
Thy fate is the common fate of all,
Into each life some rain must fall,
Some days must be dark and dreary.

Just Call

CHRISTY PHILLIPPE

"Dad, why don't you call some of your friends?" Denise asked her seventy-five-year-old father, who had recently come to live with her.

Denise's dad had seemed a little down and more than a little lonely lately, but he still kept ignoring his daughter's suggestion. Finally he admitted the reason to Denise: "I don't have anything to talk to them about."

But things changed one day when one of his old friends called him. Denise could hear her father laughing boisterously in the other room before hanging up after almost an hour.

When Denise asked what they had talked about for so long, her dad thought for a moment and then replied with a chuckle: "Well, I guess we didn't talk about much at all! It was just good to hear his voice."

The next day, Denise couldn't help but notice that the spring was back in her father's step. ☁

God Is Good

MELVA COOPER

My two-year-old granddaughter, Mary Kathryn, and I were running errands. My hand held tightly to the wheel as I maneuvered us through the traffic. Mary Kathryn sat in the rear, securely buckled in her car seat.

There was no need for conversation that day. Mary Kathryn's precious voice was ringing out with songs she had learned from Sunday school, the song in her heart springing forth and filling the van with joy. The melodies cheered my spirit as we continued our journey.

A few minutes later, I decided to share a package of M&M's with Mary Kathryn. The tiny, colorful pieces of chocolate were her favorite. While laughing and eating the M&M's, I said to her lovingly, "These M&M's are so good, aren't they?" Almost as if I had given her a cue with the word *good*, Mary Kathryn began to sing "God Is So Good." Delighted, I listened in awe as her sweet angelic voice completed the song.

Startled that she knew all of the words, I thanked God that at the tender age of two, Mary Kathryn really knew that God was good. Life as viewed from her youthful perspective was all about love.

Does the simple word good trigger in your mind the fact that "God is so good, He's so good to us"? Whether you're twenty-seven months, twenty-seven years, or perhaps nearing the age of Mary Kathryn's grandmother, you can let God's goodness engulf you. Soak it up.

He loves, honors, cherishes, esteems, values, guards, and protects you.

Amidst the trials and tribulations that confront you daily, let the song that sprang from the heart of a very young grand-daughter remind you that God is good.

> THANK THE LORD BECAUSE HE IS GOOD.
> HIS LOVE CONTINUES FOREVER.
> **1 CHRONICLES 16:34**

THE RAINY DAY BOOK

This is my "depressed stance."
When you're depressed, it makes
a lot of difference how you stand.
The worst thing you can do is
straighten up and hold your head
high because then you'll start to
feel better. If you're going to get
any joy out of being depressed,
you've got to stand like this.

CHARLIE BROWN

I'd Rather Be

HARVEY NOWLAND

Personally
I'd rather be a rambler
Than a farmer
A shepherd than a king
A wise man than wealthy
Healthy
Though without fame
I'd rather be like I am
Than to be like him or you
For that's the way
God made me
And I can live with that
Can you?

A cloudy day is no match for a sunny disposition.

WILLIAM A. WARD

Seven Quick Cures for the Rainy Day Blues

TANYA WARRINGTON

Sometimes the dark skies can bring your mood down. Next time you're facing a rainy day—or just a blue day—try one of these mood lifters:

- Take a walk in the rain or stomp in a rain puddle—just for fun.
- Put your houseplants outside for a rainwater shower.
- Buy yourself a flower. A long-lasting carnation or mum can brighten any day.
- Rent and watch the musical *Singing in the Rain* or curl up with a good book.
- Clean out a drawer or a closet.
- Light a candle or build a fire in the fireplace.
- Play your favorite music.

Lord, Why Do You Whisper?

JERRY D. LANE

Lord, speak to me.
Just don't whisper.
It's loud down here.
Phones, TV, voices—
All clamoring for attention.

The alarm goes off.
I'm tired and I snooze it.
Jump in the shower,
Grab a bagel.
Rush out the door.
I'm on my cell phone in the car.

Lord, speak to me.
Just don't whisper.
The office is busy and loud.
Lunchtime with co-workers.
Sorry I laughed at that joke.
Sorry for misusing work time.

It's time to go home.
Another rush hour.
I'm on the phone again.
Sorry I cut someone off in traffic.
Sorry I lost my temper and yelled.

Lord, speak to me.
Just don't whisper.
Now that I'm home,
Activity is non-stop.
TV when it's not.
Lord, why do You whisper?

I want to know Your will.
But I can't hear it.
I remember You speak in a still, small voice.
But it's loud down here.
Or am I just not listening?
Am I quiet long enough to hear?
Would I recognize Your voice?

Lord, whisper to me.
I'm listening.

A kind word is like a spring day.

RUSSIAN PROVERB

A Lesson in Kindness

KAYLEEN J. REUSSER

It was snowing as I finished unbuckling my baby from her car seat. A toot from behind reminded me that I was holding up traffic on the one-way street.

I didn't care. My six-month-old had to get an immunization shot, which meant she would be up all night with a fever. My head ached like I was coming down with the flu, and my husband's job didn't look steady for the holidays.

I was not in a good mood.

The truck tooted its horn again. When I finally had my little one in my arms, huddled against the cold air, I looked up and felt my heart sink. I had inadvertently parked in a delivery zone. A look at the name printed on the truck behind me confirmed that I was parked in the truck's space.

> The nearest empty place was more than a block away. Gritting my teeth, I was tempted to go home and reschedule my baby's vaccination for a day when things were going better, but I didn't.

Angry at myself for not noticing the sign sooner, I bundled my baby back into the car and looked down the street. The nearest empty place was more than a block away. Gritting my teeth, I was tempted to go home and reschedule my baby's vaccination for a day when things were going better, but I didn't.

After managing to park in a tight spot, I again got ready to get out of my car. Glancing up, I saw someone waiting for me outside. I knew it was the truck driver. Bracing myself for a verbal attack, I slowly emerged from the car.

"Sorry about that back there." A strong note of apology rang in the man's voice. I looked at him suspiciously. He was actually smiling at me.

"I saw you had a baby," he continued, "but there wasn't any other place big enough for me to pull in."

I managed to stammer my own apology, though I was completely taken aback by his friendly manner. Like Scrooge, I wondered if this was a setup.

"I'd like to give you this." The stranger held out a ceramic mug with his company's name on the side. He didn't wait for my reply, but shouted, "Merry Christmas!" and jogged away as fast as he dared on the slick pavement.

I stared after him, the mug still in my hand. As the snow continued to fall steadily around me, a warm feeling spread throughout my body, and I smiled for the first time all day.

That mug has a permanent place on my kitchen windowsill. It serves as a constant reminder to me of the way that driver showed unexpected kindness to me that day. Seeing the mug each morning as I begin my day inspires me to work on showing that same kindness and forgiveness to everyone I will meet—clerks, cashiers, complete strangers—not just at Christmas, but every day of the year. ☁

WHOEVER GIVES TO OTHERS WILL GET RICHER;
THOSE WHO HELP OTHERS WILL THEMSELVES BE HELPED.
PROVERBS 11:25

Count your gains instead of your losses,
Count your joys instead of your woes,
Count your courage instead of your fears,
Count your friends instead of your foes,
Count your health instead of your wealth,
Count on God instead of yourself.

ANONYMOUS

By a Broom Tree

1 KINGS 19:1-6

God's chosen people were in an acute period of spiritual infidelity, following after the pagan idols and customs of their neighbors.

The king of Israel, Ahab, who was supposed to be a spiritual leader and model for his people, was a huge part of the problem. He had married the beautiful and seductive Jezebel, who was an ardent worshiper of Baal, the Canaanite god of fertility, and whose religious practices included sexual orgies and human sacrifice.

Jezebel, the real power behind the throne, had her husband set up shrines and altars and import thousands of priests to spread the worship of Baal throughout the land.

God spoke to the people and called them to repentance through a prophet named Elijah. The defining moment in his battle with the priests of Baal occurred on Mount Carmel (1 Kings 18:20). In a contest to prove who was the true God, he ordered the people to prepare two bulls for sacrifice, but not set fire to them. Elijah and the prophets of Baal would each pray for fire, and "the god who answers by setting fire to his wood is the true God" (1 Kings 18:24).

For hours, the prophets of Baal prayed and performed incantations, all to no avail. At noon, Elijah called for several gallons of water to be poured over his bull. After he prayed a simple prayer, fire came down from heaven, burning the bull and evaporating the water. The people fell to the ground in worship.

One would think that after such a remarkable victory Elijah would be exultant and on top of the world. But what he soon discovered was that a furious Jezebel had put out a contract on his head, and assassins were on his heels.

He ran to the wilderness, and in a moment of despair lay against a broom tree and cried out to God that he no longer wanted to live: "'I have had enough, Lord,' he prayed. 'Let me die'" (1 Kings 19:4).

God's answer was to help Elijah sleep and send him food: "Elijah saw near his head a loaf baked over coals and a jar of water, so he ate and drank. Then he went back to sleep" (1 Kings 19:6).

There are a myriad of causes for the blues. Sometimes we need nothing more than the right food and some extra rest. The good news is that when we cry to our kind and gracious Heavenly Father, He gives us what we need most. ☁

God's Promises for Difficult Days

God will...

Give you joy and strength
The joy of the Lord will make you strong.

NEHEMIAH 8:10

Hear your prayers
I cried out to the LORD in my great trouble,
and he answered me.

JONAH 2:2

Bring about His plans for your life
It may seem like a long time,
but be patient and wait for it,
because it will surely come;
it will not be delayed.

HABAKKUK 2:3

Refresh you
He gives me new strength.
He leads me on paths that are right
for the good of his name.

PSALM 23:3

Guide you
In all your ways acknowledge Him,
And He shall direct your paths.

PROVERBS 3:6

Help you when you're tired
The Lord helps those who have been defeated
and takes care of those who are in trouble.

PSALM 145:14

Continue to work in your life
God began doing a good work in you,
and I am sure he will continue it until it
is finished when Jesus Christ comes again.

PHILIPPIANS 1:6

A Prayer for Wisdom and Strength

Dear Heavenly Father,

Today there just isn't much spring in my step. Help me remember that there are good times around the corner, that You bring gifts into my life and hold me up during difficult days. Thank You for sending people to encourage me and make me laugh.

Lord, please use this blue day to make me more aware of You in my life.

SUNSHINY DAYS

*Laughter is the sun that drives winter
from the human face.*

VICTOR HUGO

*Wow! What a beautiful day. From the deep green of the grass to the cobalt blue of
the sky, vibrant colors are everywhere.*

I guess if it never rained, I might be tempted to take a day like today for granted.

Within the seasons of the soul, thank God, for He is faithful in all
circumstances. When the storms rage, God is there. And when the sun
shines brightly on an early summer day—or in your life—we have one more
vivid reminder that storms pass, but God's love always endures.

Maybe it's time today to hearken to the old advice to "stop and smell the
roses." And "Spread a Little Sunshine" offers some great tips on how to
brighten others' days as well.

THE LORD GOD IS LIKE A SUN AND SHIELD;
THE LORD GIVES US KINDNESS AND HONOR.
HE DOES NOT HOLD BACK ANYTHING GOOD
FROM THOSE WHOSE LIVES ARE INNOCENT.

PSALM 84:11

When you look at your life, the greatest happinesses are family happinesses.

JOYCE BROTHERS

Just Between Us

JANET LYNN MITCHELL

I wish I could have seen his face when he answered the phone. Even though I was married to Marty, I still called home when I needed him.

"Dad, my garage door broke."

"Well, do you need me to pick up a new spring?"

"No. I think I kinda need you to come over. You see, I had places to go and people to see, so when I couldn't pull out like usual, I...sort of tried to turn my van around."

"You did what?"

"I tried to turn my van around, you know, like a U-turn. I tried to turn the van and head out the other garage door!" I confessed while stifling my giggles.

For a moment there was silence. I could imagine my father

"Dad, it's like this. My van is stuck in my garage. Sideways."

sitting in his favorite chair, his brow furrowed as he tried to picture what his youngest daughter had attempted. While he thought, I assessed my situation and concluded there was no way I wanted my husband to come home from work and see my creative attempt to get to the mall.

Eventually, my father's thoughts broke into words. "Honey, did you make it out the other door? What exactly do you need me to do?"

I took a deep breath and tried to find an appropriate way to break the news, yet nothing came to mind. As I had done my entire life, I swallowed and then presented my problem to my father.

"Dad, it's like this. My van is stuck in my garage."

"Stuck?"

"Yeah. Stuck. Sideways."

"Sideways?"

"Dad, I thought I could turn it around. I started backing up and going forward, trying to maneuver it around so that I could exit out of the second garage door. I had a full tank of gas and I was doing a good job of getting it out myself until now. Anyway, can you come over and help me before Marty gets home from work?"

My dad knew I often thought outside the box. In fact, he'd been one to believe in my dreams, support my attempts, and praise my accomplishments.

Within minutes, my dad had left his chair and was standing in my garage surveying my dilemma. He scratched his head, placed his hands on his hips, and assured me that he had "never seen such." Then without saying a word, yet wearing a grin that hinted, "Now I've seen it all," he crawled into the driver's seat and began inching his way, slowly turning the van.

I crawled up onto the workbench and watched. My dad caught my eye and gave me a wink. Holding my hand over my mouth, I tried to control my laughter as my father repeatedly drove my van three feet forward then three feet in reverse, while maneuvering the steering wheel. I thought of Marty surprising me, coming home early, finding his father-in-law "driving" in his garage and me cheering him on with passion!

Instantly, I flashed back to the many times my dad had come to my rescue, not questioning me as to the how or why of my predicament, but concentrating on the "what now" and the solution. It was no secret—my dad knew that I often thought, shall we say, "outside the box." In fact, he'd been one to believe in my dreams, support my attempts, and praise my accomplishments.

As I watched him vigorously turn the steering wheel, I pondered his patience, wisdom, and endless love for me. Today was just an ordinary day. I knew for certain, no matter what, that I could always call on my dad. I knew that I was loved and my father knew that I loved him.

An hour before Marty arrived home, my father beamed as he drove the van out the second garage door and parked it in the driveway. I walked out to meet him, applauding, and he rolled down the window.

"Problem solved," he said.

"Just between us?" I asked in a coy request that this would remain our little secret.

"Between us," he nodded. "Yep, this one is going to have to be just between us, as no one would ever believe it!"

I THANK MY GOD EVERY TIME I REMEMBER YOU.

PHILIPPIANS 1:3

*Give thanks to the
Lord because he is good.
His love continues forever.*

PSALM 136:1

Count Your Blessings

The best thing about sunny days is that they remind us that gloomy days are only temporary. Take a minute to list fifty things that are great about your life (and the more trouble you have with this exercise, the more you need to do it!). Tuck your list somewhere safe, and refer to it when you need a reminder that a sunny day is just around the corner.

Ever notice how tense grown-ups get when they're recreating?

BILL WATTERSON, CALVIN AND HOBBES

The Call of the Wild

KATHRYN LAY

I grew up a city gal. My idea of camping was staying in a hotel with no cable. I do enjoy the beauty and serenity of the country—long walks, open spaces, lots of trees and flowers all around me.

But I never claimed to be an expert on country life.

I loved the beauty of nature that God has created, but I preferred it bug-free, snake-free, and poison ivy-free. I liked my nature clean, safe, and non-scary. My new husband kept telling me that I was missing out on the true excitement of the outdoors that God had given us.

> I loved the beauty of nature that God has created, but I preferred it bug-free, snake-free, and poison ivy-free. I liked my nature clean, safe, and non-scary.

While on our first real vacation as man and wife, we took a trip to the hill country of Texas. We stopped at the LBJ Ranch to catch a glimpse of life in the country.

I enjoyed the beautiful wildflowers that Ladybird Johnson loved and planted throughout the area. There were birds singing in the trees and lazy clouds in the sky. This seemed like the orderly, tame nature I felt comfortable with. God's handiwork flooded my vision and Vivaldi cello tunes danced in my head.

We toured a pioneer-style home, listening to talks about canning, weaving, and washing clothes in a time without supermarkets, malls, or washing machines. We strolled through the garden, and I imagined growing my own fresh vegetables.

A guide led us and a small crowd of tourists along a gravelly path through a canopy of trees. A winding stream trickled slowly several feet below us. My husband pointed out the bright red cardinal that sat almost hidden in a tree. I held my breath as I positioned my camera for just the right shot. A wild rabbit shot past us when we frightened it. I sighed in contentment.

What was that? A bear? A cougar? Were there wolves in this part of Texas?

No loud cars, ringing phones, blaring televisions. Just me and nature.

"Hey, look at that," my husband said, pointing toward the stream.

The others in the group moved closer to the edge and peered into the stream.

I looked, expecting to see a beautiful water bird or comical turtle sitting by the stream. Instead, we watched a snake chasing a small fish. I squealed and backed away.

"Isn't God amazing?" my husband said. "Look at the way that snake moves."

I had no intention of admiring the snake as it chased down its dinner.

This part of nature was beginning to reach the edge of my limits of the enjoyable outdoors.

I turned and nearly ran into sticky strands stretched across the branches of a tree. A long-legged yellow and black spider waited lazily for a meal to find his web.

I shuddered and imagined bugs hidden all around me, waiting to pounce. Couldn't my husband understand we were invading an alien world? Sure, God created all things—including this city girl, who was completely out of her element.

"Don't overreact," my husband whispered. "Just enjoy the things you aren't used to seeing in the city."

"Hey, I'm not completely ignorant about the country," I defended myself. "I know what's dangerous and what isn't."

Then, from the shadows came a sound. I grabbed my husband's arm. "What's that? A bear? A cougar?" Were there wolves in this part of Texas?

There were snickers from the tour guide and the other tourists, who perhaps were not as citified as I.

My husband laughed.

"What's that noise?" I said again, angry at his lack of concern. Were we about to be attacked in this serene setting? "Is it a coyote? Should we climb a tree?"

Richard patted my arm. "No," he said. "It's a rooster."

I listened again to the threatening sound. It was a rooster. But it could've been a predator.

We finished the tour and headed back to our hotel. I flipped on the television and searched until I found a show about a man journeying through swamps and forests, studying the wildlife and photographing the beauty God had created.

I leaned back on the comfortable hotel bed and looked around me. No bugs. No snakes. No weird noises. I was enjoying God's nature without one scary rooster to distract me. ☁

GOD RICHLY GIVES US EVERYTHING TO ENJOY.

1 TIMOTHY 6:17

Spread a Little Sunshine

NANCY B. GIBBS

One warm spring morning, I was riding down a highway and noticed a creek alongside the road. A tree had fallen over the water, and the sunshine was bearing down on it, making it a prime sunning spot. Turtles lined the tree, taking up every exposed inch of the trunk. The reptiles were basking in the warmth of the sunlight as if they were waiting for a magnificent morning show to begin.

I thought about how we humans oftentimes get too busy to bask in the sunlight or appreciate the beauty of each new day. We're often too busy to appreciate the sunshine in our own lives, much less reflect rays of happiness to those we meet. Here are ten easy ways to spread sunshine to others and say you care:

- Compliment others for their accomplishments and efforts.
- Smile at everyone you meet.
- Say a sincere "good morning" to make others realize that you care for them.
- Shake hands—a nice, firm handshake says, "You are important."
- Send out a "thinking of you" note every day for a week to a friend or coworker.
- Invite someone to visit your church and offer to pick them up.
- When you bake bread, take a loaf to a shut-in while it's still warm.

- Say "I love you" often.

- Invite a neighbor over for coffee or tea.

- Pray for your family and friends each day.

When we spread rays of the sunshine to those around us, we can't help but be warmed by the light. Although we should give for the sake of giving rather than for selfish reasons, the truth is that when we give, the light of generosity always bounces back to us.

I THINK YOU MIGHT
DISPENSE WITH HALF YOUR
DOCTORS IF YOU WOULD ONLY
CONSULT DR. SUN MORE.

HENRY WARD BEECHER

They Said It

Wherever you go, no matter what the weather,
always bring your own sunshine.

ANTHONY J. D'ANGELO

A positive attitude may not solve all your problems,
but it will annoy enough people to make it worth the effort.

HERM ALBRIGHT

I have found that if you love life, life will love you back.

ARTHUR RUBINSTEIN

Today I live in the quiet, joyous expectation of good.

ERNEST HOLMEN

There are some days when I think I'm going
to die from an overdose of satisfaction.

SALVADOR DALI

Enjoy the little things, for one day you may
look back and realize they were the big things.

ROBERT BRAULT

Chivalry Is Not Dead

KATIE MINTER JONES

"And I thought chivalry was dead," I remarked to my sister-in-law as we watched a teenage boy carry his girlfriend over a puddle.

Our families piled into our cars to head home after our day at the park. In the car, one of my four-year-old twin sons asked, "Mama, how did you know that girl?"

"What girl?" I responded.

"That girl at the park."

I thought for a moment then said, "I don't know which girl you're talking about."

He sighed loudly as he explained, "You know—Chivalry. You thought she was dead."

*I love to think of nature
as an unlimited
broadcasting station,
through which God
speaks to us every hour,
if we will only tune in.*

GEORGE WASHINGTON CARVER

Catching God's Grace

STAN MEEK

Mornings at our hideaway home in northeast Oklahoma are always fresh as a newly-laid egg. Today was no exception. The crowing rooster down the street awakened sleeping memories from my early childhood days on the family farm.

This spring day dawned in splendor after a cool night of fifty degrees. Not a cloud was in the sky. The quiet was unbroken by the gentle breeze that stirred the grass. The dewy air was just the right temperature, and a brown thrasher gave a free concert entitled "Festival of Song" (they sing like mockingbirds, you know).

All day long, this proud thrasher paraded his talents, changing his position only occasionally to ensure that every creature in this theater of glory could revel in his exhibition of melodies. Later, he shared the spotlight with a cardinal or two, yet seemed determined to be the star performer of this day.

> This spring day dawned in splendor after a cool night of fifty degrees. Not a cloud was in the sky. The quiet was unbroken by the gentle breeze that stirred the grass. The dewy air was just the right temperature, and a brown thrasher gave a free concert entitled "Festival of Song."

My wife, Pat, and I walked east up and down the roller-coaster hills leading to the lake bluff. We were accompanied by the neighbor's dog, Sandy. She thinks she's our dog too. It was "Sandy's Sabbath"—that's what her owners always say when Sandy comes to visit "the preacher."

We descended the big hollow, so deep you can't see the bottom until you are nearly halfway down. Then, with energy bursting in our arms and legs, we climbed the other side to the crest of the bluff. Just where Cardinal Road runs into Quail Run Road, the view of Lake Hudson was breathtaking. The air was invigorating. We inhaled deeply during our brisk walk, enjoying this royal revelry.

Is God not all around us? Are we not immersed in grace? Is grace not in the air we breathe?

Each day, now, the trees seem to be robed in ever richer, greener attire. If you listen carefully, they are shouting, "Grace is found here. See, winter is not forever. Life will be rich and beautiful again."

Perhaps we are accustomed to finding grace only in stories of God's work in people's lives, but does grace always have to wear a face? Can't we trace the mystery of grace in the everyday world around us? Doesn't a day like today bring the soft touch of sovereign appealings to my spirit?

Must grace be so loudly and boldly spiritual—spectacular interventions, radical conversions, dramatic healings? Is God not all around us? Are we not immersed in grace? Is grace not in the air we breathe? Coasting on the wings of the butterfly that floats from the daffodils to the creeping phlox? Buzzing around us in the ruby-throated hummingbird, his muted motor propelling him like a helicopter around our feeders and honeysuckle?

This is not pantheism or worship of the world. It is awareness. Hush! God, the world-maker, is speaking to my soul. The apostle wrote: "For since the creation of the world His invisible attributes are clearly seen, being understood by the things that are made, even His eternal power and Godhead" (Romans 1:20 NKJV).

As I thought about my day, I felt as Annie Dillard did when she wrote in *Pilgrim at Tinker Creek* about the simple joys of "patting a puppy," and "seeing the flames of the falling sun on distant cedar trees." She exclaimed, "This is it, this is it; praise the Lord, praise the Lord."

Oh, I'll admit that it isn't in the same category as exulting, "Praise the Lord," when feeling free from guilt and sin, or when feeling loved and accepted by God even when you've blown it, but the world around us has enough grace in it to awaken those with any spiritual receptivity at all. You can catch some of this grace too, if your heart is open.

Dillard says, "You catch grace as a man fills his cup at a waterfall." Perhaps she's right. For Pat and me this has been a waterfall day. Thank You, Lord, for filling our cups. Thank You for being found in the middle of ordinary days. ☁

THE HEAVENS TELL THE GLORY OF GOD,
AND THE SKIES ANNOUNCE
WHAT HIS HANDS HAVE MADE.

PSALM 19:1

Make a Joyful Noise

PSALM 100

God's joy is a powerful, dynamic force that lifts one's spirit, imparts courage and wisdom, and becomes an expression of a miracle inside of us that speaks to the world of God's goodness and kindness.

Great men and women of faith in God's word were not sheltered from life's troubles and storms, but they did find ways to express the joy of knowing God.

- David, a fugitive and on the run from a madman, was quick to declare: "Be exalted, O God, above the heavens; let Your glory be above all the earth" (Psalm 57:5 NKJV).

- Mary, a young teen virgin who had almost lost her betrothed and reputation while bearing God's Son, said, "My soul praises the Lord; my heart rejoices in God my Savior" (Luke 1:46-47).

- Hannah, who was tormented for years because she couldn't bear children, was finally granted a son, and promptly gave him back to God while praying, "The Lord has filled my heart with joy; I feel very strong in the Lord. I can laugh at my enemies; I am glad because you have helped me!" (1 Samuel 2:1).

- Stephen, the first Christian martyr, at the hour of his death, even as the first stone was being cast, smiled toward heaven and joyfully marveled, "Look! I see heaven open and the Son of Man standing at God's right side" (Acts 7:56).

🌢 Stephen's state of grace haunted a young persecutor named Saul, who would be renamed Paul, and who faced a myriad of hardships in service to God and others, yet could declare: "Be full of joy in the Lord always. I will say again, be full of joy" (Philippians 4:4).

Whether your life is filled with good things or troubles right now, you too can "make a joyful noise" (Psalm 66:1) as you come into the presence of God with joy and thanksgiving. ☁

> BUT LET EVERYONE WHO TRUSTS YOU BE HAPPY;
> LET THEM SING GLAD SONGS FOREVER.
>
> **PSALM 5:11**

God's Promises for Sunny Days

God will...

Give you good things
No good thing will He withhold
From those who walk uprightly.

PSALM 84:11 NKJV

Give you what you need to enjoy life
You give us wine that makes happy hearts
and olive oil that makes our faces shine.
You give us bread that gives us strength.

PSALM 104:15

Be found by you as you seek Him
You will search for me.
And when you search for me with
all your heart, you will find me!

JEREMIAH 29:13

Lighten your burdens

Accept my teachings and learn from me,
because I am gentle and humble
in spirit, and you will find rest for your lives.
The teaching that I ask you to accept is easy;
the load I give you to carry is light.

MATTHEW 11:29-30

Give you joy

I have set the Lord always before me;
Because He is at my right hand I shall not be moved.
Therefore my heart is glad, and my glory rejoices;
My flesh also will rest in hope.

PSALM 16:8-9 NKJV

Give good and perfect gifts

Every good action and every perfect gift is from God.

JAMES 1:17

Bless you abundantly

You prepare a meal for me in front of my enemies.
You pour oil on my head; you fill my cup to overflowing.

PSALM 23:5

A Prayer of Gratitude and Joy

Dear Heavenly Father,

Thank You, Lord, for bringing just the right amount of rain and sun into my life. Thank You for Your grace, for sending blessings my way at just the right time. Thank You for Your goodness.

Today, give me a new sense of gratitude to You for the many ways You have blessed my life.

SPRINKLES ON A HOT DAY

Seize from every moment its unique novelty,
and do not prepare your joys.

ANDRÉ GIDE

Aaaah. A blistering hot day. A long hike. A cool refreshing drink of water. A few sprinkles drop from the sky and give relief.

My parched throat finds relief and I am happy and content. How could I have even complained about a rainy day?

"Rain, rain, go away, come again another day"—be careful what you wish for. Just as arid farmland in the nation's breadbasket aches for even a sprinkle of rain, so the soil of our hearts is renewed by all of the experiences God brings or allows into our lives.

We gain perspective, compassion, determination, resilience, and reliance on God as we embrace and enjoy the sunny and rainy days alike.

Sure there are days we could have missed and never missed, but all of our days are part of the journey to becoming more and more like Jesus.

Savor and delight as you read Nancy B. Gibbs' advice on how to have a wacky day and the story of how Janet Lynn Mitchell learned to cut loose and have a good time in the midst of difficulties. Today may be a scorcher for you—but who knows what little serendipities are just waiting to bring refreshment and joy to your life?

GOD, YOU SENT MUCH RAIN; YOU REFRESHED YOUR TIRED LAND.

PSALM 68:9

For daily need there is daily grace; for sudden need, sudden grace, and for overwhelming need, overwhelming grace.

JOHN BLANCHARD

The Small Things of God

JAY COOKINGHAM

On one summer vacation in North Carolina, my daughter was swimming in the surf and lost a favorite bracelet. After searching and coming up empty handed, she was devastated. We talked and prayed about God's love for her, even in the small things. We left the beach for lunch and the bracelet in God's hands.

Around sunset, we returned to the beach for a walk, and as my daughter was looking for shells, I went to cool my feet in the water. As I stepped into the waves, something rolled up between my feet. Shiny pink beads shone in the wet sand—could it be? Sure enough, it was Kim's bracelet.

I picked up the once lost treasure and called to my daughter. When she ran over, I ceremoniously placed the trinket back into her hands, awed by God's tender concern.

Have a Wacky Day!

NANCY B. GIBBS

Our lives can get so full, so tightly organized and structured, that we can forget how to have fun. To enjoy life, sometimes we have to transform our ordinary days into extraordinary days. Sometimes we have to act a little wacky if we want to laugh. So go ahead and have a wacky day! Here are a dozen starters.

- Instead of the usual cereal or eggs, eat pizza or spaghetti for breakfast.

- Go to the park and swing. To add to the fun, take along a friend to push you.

- Get up early in the morning and drive across your state, with no place to go. Stop at every spot that looks interesting and enjoy the scenery. Don't forget the picnic lunch.

- Have a progressive dinner. Go to one restaurant for a small salad. Move on to another for a couple of veggies. Then try out a new cafeteria and a new entrée (something you have never had the nerve to try before). Last but not least, stop at another restaurant for dessert.

- Tune in to the shopping network. You will discover products you never knew existed.

- Stay overnight in the hotel down the street. Have you ever wondered what the rooms looked like? This will be your chance to find out. (As an added benefit, the kids can go swimming or play in the game room.)

- If it's a nice day and your workplace is nearby, ride your bike to work.

- Start out the day looking for at least three people to help and do something kind for each of them. Beware: This may become habit forming.

- Pay for the driver's meal in the car behind you at a fast-food restaurant. You will laugh all the way home.

- Spend the entire day at the library reading and drinking coffee or cappuccino.

- If possible, go to work with your mate. You will know more about what he or she does all day.

- Exchange household tasks with your kids—you take over their jobs for one day, and have them take over yours. You will all have fun doing something different for a change (and everything will still get done).

Go ahead—pick a date, mark it on the calendar, and have a wacky day! ☁

Whence comes this idea that if what we are doing is fun, it can't be God's will? The God who made giraffes, a baby's fingernails, a puppy's tail, a crooknecked squash, the bobwhite's call, and a young girl's giggle, has a sense of humor. Make no mistake about that.

CATHERINE MARSHALL

*What soap
is to the body,
laughter is
to the soul.*

YIDDISH PROVERB

Three Scoops High

JANET LYNN MITCHELL

It had been months since Marty and I had gone out on a date or done something fun with our kids. Our son Joel had been born prematurely, and our days of staying out late were indefinitely suspended.

While he was still in the hospital, our kindergartener, Jenna Marie, was hospitalized with juvenile diabetes. The past year had included thirteen hospitalizations and lots of stress. Even though things were settling down—baby Joel was home now and using an apnea monitor, Jenna was adjusting to her four shots a day, and four-year-old Jason was happy that his life was returning to normal—we braced ourselves for the next "whatever." Marty and I knew that somehow we needed to lighten the tension we all felt. We needed some time with friends. We needed a little fun.

> Even though things were settling down, we braced ourselves for the next "whatever." Marty and I knew that somehow we needed to lighten the tension we all felt. We needed some time with friends. We needed a little fun.

One afternoon, it struck me. I giggled as I began to tell Marty my idea. With a wink of his eye and a nod of his head, I knew he was game. Immediately, we called Jenna and Jason.

"How would you like to have a slumber party?" Marty asked them after they ran in from outside.

"A what?" Jason replied, not having a clue what his father was talking about.

"It's a sleepover party," I explained.

"A party?" Jenna shouted.

"Yeah, let's have a party!" Jason agreed while giving Jenna a high-five.

Within minutes, I was on the phone calling two of our friends. After they filled me in on the goings-on in their lives, I invited their kids (ages ranging from four to six) to our family slumber party the next Friday night. "Look at it this way. We'll have your kids, and you guys can go out on a date!"

The kids piled out and gathered around Marty and me. Opening the bags that we held, Marty and I handed each child a roll of toilet paper. "What do we do with this?" Matthew asked, perplexed.

Over the next few days, Marty, the kids, and I planned our slumber party. Jason found and dusted off our "party box," which held the odds and ends from parties of our past. Soon party hats, blowers, and balloons honoring every occasion covered our floor. The kids carefully selected a hat for each partier. "Will Joel want a hat?" Jason asked me. "Sure," I replied. After all, everyone should be in on the fun.

Before the night was over, a tablecloth covered the table, set with Barney plates, baseball napkins, and Christmas cups, along with Barbie and Scooby Doo hats and clown-shaped noisemakers.

"It's perfect!" Jenna exulted proudly.

"Yeah, now we just need the kids!" Jason exclaimed.

The kids' excitement was like electricity running through our home the day before the party, and Marty and I had a sparkle in our eyes. When

Friday night came, our guests ran our doorbell, grinning and towing sleeping bags. Their parents were delighted to have the night off for some extra fun themselves.

Marty helped the kids lay out their sleeping bags in domino rows in the living room, then took them out to the backyard to play tag while I ordered the pizza. When the pizza was delivered, the kids noisily found a seat at the "party table" and put on their hats. Even Joel wore a hat. "We're celebrating everything!" Jennifer said, surveying the multiple themes that graced our table.

"Tonight we're celebrating friends," I added.

In between bites of pizza, the kids giggled and told stories. Marty was the hit of the party as he told every joke he knew.

Once the kids were finished, they moved on to the living room and watched a video while I cleaned up. Moments before the movie ended, I gathered the needed "materials" for our next activity while Marty scooped ice cream into bowls—three scoops high. We set the ice cream, topped with brightly colored sprinkles, on the table and called the kids. Once the ice cream was gone, Marty and I knew it was time.

"Grab your coats," he shouted to the kids while I grabbed the video camera. "We're going for a ride." We piled into our cars.

"Where are we going? What are we going to do?" echoed from the backseat. I could hardly contain my giggles. I knew just where we were going and why.

"Hey, this is my house!" Matthew hollered as we drove by.

"You're right—and we're about to decorate it!" I said as I drove down the street and parked around the corner.

The kids piled out and gathered around Marty and me. Opening the bags that we held, Marty and I handed each child a roll of toilet paper. "What do we do with this?" Matthew asked, perplexed.

"We're going to surprise your parents and decorate your houses. You know—wrap them like a present in toilet paper," I explained.

Marty then gave the instructions. "You can decorate the grass, the trees, and even the mailboxes. But when you see the lights of a car heading down the street, you either need to hit the ground and lay flat on the grass, or you can freeze in place and pretend you're a tree."

Immediately laughter and hysteria broke out. The kids couldn't believe that we had brought them to do something so outrageous.

Marty gave the word and the kids began to "decorate." He even showed them a few tricks he'd learned as a teenager. With a "Well done!" from my husband, we finished Matt's house and headed off to house number two.

You can only imagine the surprise when our friends found our "gift of love" spread across their front lawns. I can still hear the laughter from the following morning when we took the children back to clean up the fun. After the yards were spotless, we handed their parents proof—a videotape of our family slumber party, ice cream with sprinkles scooped three scoops high, and their children acting like trees.

Yes, Marty and I needed to ease the tension in our home, and our kids simply needed time with friends and a chance to have some outrageous fun! We did—and it was a night to remember. ☁

WORRY IS A HEAVY LOAD, BUT A
KIND WORD CHEERS YOU UP.

PROVERBS 12:25

Shake Things Up

If you're feeling bogged down or stressed, maybe you need a reminder that life is all about the little things. Instead of eating lunch at your desk or grabbing fast food, why not go to an ice cream place for lunch or order a sweet, fluffy coffee drink to go with your usual sandwich? Or, if you don't want to load up on all that sugar, use your usual lunchtime to call friends just to say hi or organize a game night with your loved ones. Whatever you decide to do, take a minute to thank God for those little fun things that make life great.

Joke Break

These may be the worst jokes yet. They're inexcusably bad, really. But you know you're going to read them—and probably read them to someone else.

When it rains cats and dogs, what does a vet step into?
Poodles.

What do you get when you cross poison ivy with a four-leaf clover?
A rash of good luck.

What's raised during the rainy season in Brazil?
Umbrellas.

How many different kinds of gnus are there?
Two: good gnus and bad gnus.

Mirth is God's medicine.
Everybody ought to bathe in it.

HENRY WARD BEECHER

He gives rain
to the earth
and sends water
on the fields.

JOB 5:10

The Benefits of Water

You've heard it a thousand times before: You need water. It's true—being sufficiently hydrated carries many health benefits.

- Keeping hydrated increases your mental sharpness and wards off dehydration-related headaches and fatigue.
- Research consistently shows that drinking plenty of water keeps your heart and digestive system healthy and may even prevent a variety of cancers.
- Thirst pangs are often mistaken for hunger pains, and drinking lots of water has long been prescribed as an aid to maintaining body weight.

The standard guideline for water intake is eight glasses of water a day, but no one ever said it's easy to drink that much water. It takes effort. Corey, a physical therapist who knows the importance of staying hydrated, fills eight eight-ounce disposable cups with cool water and lines them up on the windowsill in his office each morning. He drinks them one after another throughout the day, motivated by the knowledge that if he waits to drink them all until 5:15 in the evening, he'll have to drive home a little faster than he'd like.

Especially during hot, dry times, give your body what it needs—and thank God that He always gives you what you need.

The most popular
do-it-yourself kits
will always be a
checkbook and
a ballpoint pen.

AUTHOR UNKNOWN

For the Love of Tools

CANDY ARRINGTON

Could someone give me a little help here?" The somewhat urgent bellow came from a distant corner of the house.

Thinking only "medical emergency," son, daughter, and I dashed from separate rooms, colliding in the hall. We discovered him in the bedroom. There was no blood, no contorted limbs. Instead, the sight that greeted us was my husband precariously perched with one foot in a chair and one foot on the bed, pouring buckets of sweat and squinting at the guts to the ceiling fan dangling overhead.

"Someone hold this for me," he said, gesturing to the tangled mass of hanging wires and light bulbs. The kids and I looked at each other with you-do-it faces. In a moment of great bravery, our daughter stepped up onto the bed to assist her father.

"What are you doing?" I ventured.

"Fixing the fan," he replied. I wondered if he wanted to tack a "duh" on the end of that statement.

There are pans, rollers, long-stick handles, sponges, brushes, and cans from last year's painting project; never-installed plastic corner protectors for the wallpaper drooping in the corner; and a huge set of Allen (I think) wrenches in a bulky plastic suitcase-looking thing that were a necessity on some occasion.

"What's wrong with it? I mean, besides being apart like that."

"The chain came out several weeks ago. It's stuck on low and I'm going to fix it."

I knew it was risky, but I asked anyway. "Do you know how?"

"It shouldn't be that hard now that I've got the thing apart," he said.

But I remembered from numerous other home repair fiascos that the problem comes not in the taking apart, but in the reassembling.

Using unparalleled restraint, I zipped my lip, nodded, and beat a hasty retreat to the laundry room, a safe haven during bouts of the fixits. As I went, I thought I heard him utter those dreaded words, "But I'm not sure I have the right tools."

Have you ever noticed how men pick the most unusual times to tackle fixit tasks? Here we were at 10:00 on a Wednesday night, dog-tired from church activities and needing to wind down, but my husband had chosen this unlikely time and was now deep into the project. I listened for further commands, falling bodies, or footsteps on the stairs as I folded clothes. It was inevitable. Surely this project would require a midnight run to Lowe's or Wal-Mart. We never seem to have the necessary items for repairs, even though, over the years, we have acquired a garage full of tools, most with one-time use.

There are pans, rollers, long-stick handles, sponges, brushes, and cans from last year's painting project; never-installed plastic corner protectors for the wallpaper drooping in the corner; and a huge set of Allen (I think) wrenches in a bulky plastic suitcase-looking thing that were a necessity on some occasion. (Ever wonder who Mr. Allen was and if he wanted a set of wrenches named after him?)

Then there's the rubber hammer—a contradiction in terms—that we couldn't live without. Don't forget the 1960-something Boy Scout hatchet and sleeping bag that I'm afraid to touch for fear that it houses all sorts of critters.

Next to the sleeping bag sit four—no, five—car clean-and-shine kits and several rusty cans of bug and tar remover behind the gallon jugs of windshield washer fluid. Let's not forget boxes of various size nails and two electric screwdrivers charging themselves into a frenzy on the wall. The toolbox is there also. But somehow the contents are guilty of disorderly conduct as they refuse to stay in their designated slots and migrate to unlikely locations in other parts of the house and garage.

One section of our car park is dedicated to lawn and garden tools. Hoes, shovels, rakes, brooms, and a weed eater languish in profusion in a dusty corner. Although seldom used, they certainly look industrious. Last, but surely not least, are bags of end caps, brackets, and hooks for the hanger shelf, which regularly falls off the laundry room wall. (I know that wouldn't happen if I ironed more often, but this rambling isn't about my shortcomings.)

Interrupting my mental garage equipment inventory, my husband yelled a request for new light bulbs. Failing to produce the correct size and shape from the overflowing bulb box, I trudged upstairs empty-handed. "Sorry, honey, I'm afraid you'll have to buy some. We don't have anything that fits."

Our son now assisted his father as he stood on the bed and screwed the last screws into the reassembled fan. Both father and son got that faraway tool-purchasing look in their eyes as they scrambled to find their shoes.

"We'll only be a minute. We'll get light bulbs and maybe a few other things."

A sigh escaped my lips as Junior and Senior Mr. Fixit headed for the car. Somehow, I think the fan was never really broken and it was all a ploy to embark on a nocturnal tool acquisition outing. I'd better make room on the shelf. I feel another set of something taking up residence in our garage.

Books that Hug You

TERRA HANGEN

For times when you need a little bit of silly, here are a few comfort books that will entertain you and lighten your heart with whimsy and wisdom.

- Barbara Johnson's books are so spirit-lifting that you can get a chuckle just by reading the covers: *Splashes of Joy in the Cesspools of Life*, *Stick a Geranium in Your Hat and Be Happy*, *Somewhere Between Estrogen and Death*. Her books deal with life's biggest difficulties, like death, estrangement, and illness, yet her super funny bone shows up on each page through cartoons and one-sentence chuckles, and she always brings our focus back to our caring God.

- *Tears of the Giraffe* by Alexander McCall Smith. This second installment in Smith's series featuring the incomparable Mma Ramotswe, founder of the No. 1 Ladies Detective Agency, is sure to make you smile. Yes, she solves mysteries, but it is the life and times of her friends and neighbors in small-town Africa that will delight you and gently lift your spirits.

- *View from a Sketchbook*. These subtle watercolors by Marjolein Bastin and text by Tovah Martin will lead you to peaceful daydreaming. Marjolein may be familiar to you from her special line of greeting cards featuring dragonflies, paintbrushes, and everything country.

🌢 *Fuzzy Logic: A Guide to Life's Little Challenges.* For a few giggles, turn to this book with words and paintings by Jan Seabrook. Suitable for anyone who appreciates a lighthearted touch, this tiny book pairs short, witty quips with affectionate paintings of animals. Watch for quotes like "If at first you do succeed, try not to look too astonished" and "You'll always be my best friend. You know too much."

🌢 Speaking of animals, all pet lovers would do well to check out *James Herriot's Dog Stories* and *James Herriot's Cat Stories.* Filled with warm-hearted humor, each anecdotal chapter can be read quickly for a short day brightener.

Comfort books are great therapy for many of life's minor bumps and detours, and are ideal gifts for friends or family—or yourself. As Scripture reminds us, "God will yet fill your mouth with laughter and your lips with shouts of joy" (Job 8:21). ☁

Hugs are the universal medicine.

AUTHOR UNKNOWN

Hugs

GARY STANLEY

My dad was a hugger. A gentle giant, he could put his arm around you, and that simple act made the world a safer place. He always sensed when I needed to be enfolded in his arms—to know that I was safe and loved, that I belonged. He hugged me all the time.

Mom wasn't much of a hugger. My folks didn't fit the norm. His was the tender heart. Her heart was more carefully kept. Oh, she had a playful heart, taught dance, and was gifted in the bodily art of movement and grace. But she didn't understand the ways of hugging at the level Dad did. Her own dad had died during the influenza epidemic of 1919; she was two years old at the time (Aunt Judy was four, and Uncle John was only six days old). Daddy hugs aren't a part of her conscious memory. She's still learning how to translate all the love inside her into the embrace of a hug.

She let Dad in, and the cares of the day began to dissipate like a static charge running down a grounding wire. It wasn't long before the three of us were in a group hug in the middle of the kitchen with our dog Waddles dancing around our feet.

And so Dad initiated most of the hugs in our home.

I remember one day when Mom came home from work tired and frustrated. She was a first-grade teacher, and a room full of six-year-olds had "done her in." It was one of those days when she'd had no opportunity to get rid of the toxin of prolonged aggravation—you know, that feeling of being nibbled to death by ducks. Mom banged the cabinet doors and started to simmer something on the stove. Several things were coming to a rolling boil in the kitchen that afternoon.

Time to get out of the way, I thought.

Dad followed me downstairs and stood in the doorway. "Looks like thirty first graders have taken a toll on Mom today. I suspect we wouldn't have fared any better. Let's give her a hug!"

Dad was much more hopeful than I that a hug would help, so we marched upstairs to embrace a mother who didn't want to be embraced at that particular moment. He stepped into her personal space and unlocked the chains around her tense heart. To Mom's credit, she didn't bolt and bar the walls erected around her. She let Dad in, and the cares of the day began to dissipate like a static charge running down a grounding wire. It wasn't long before the three of us were in a group hug in the middle of the kitchen with our dog Waddles dancing around our feet.

Of all the hugs I ever saw or got, the ones Dad gave Mom have meant the most. Knowing that people in my family loved each other and showed it made my home a safe place. And my dad's example taught me that of all the things that make life wonderful and the cares of the world lighter, love is the greatest.

SO THESE THREE THINGS CONTINUE FOREVER: FAITH, HOPE, AND LOVE. AND THE GREATEST OF THESE IS LOVE.

1 CORINTHIANS 13:13

A good laugh and a long sleep are the best cures in the doctor's book.

IRISH PROVERB

The Woman at the Well

JOHN 4:4-42

If ever there was a person who faced difficult days, it was the woman who met Jesus at the well as recorded in John 4. Plenty of factors conspired to cause her to struggle with self-image and generally make life harder.

First of all, she was a Samaritan. In Jesus' day, the Jews despised all Samaritans as religious infidels and "half breeds." When Israel was conquered by the Babylonians in 586 B.C., the youngest and most educated were taken into captivity. When their descendants returned to Jerusalem seventy years later, they expected to find a thriving center of worship and faith. Instead, many who had been left behind converted to other religions and married people from other countries. They were despised from that moment on.

Second, she was a woman, which meant she had second-class status in her culture and was viewed as the "property" of her husband.

Third, she had failed at love. Jesus asked her where her husband was. She admitted she wasn't married, but was living with a man. Jesus pointed out she had previously been married six times! Whether a serial widow or divorcee, she had probably given up on marital vows.

Fourth, she was rejected by her peers. Jesus met her during the hottest time of the day with no one else around her. The women of Middle East villages gathered water at the well together during the coolest part of the day.

If anyone had reason to feel bad about themselves and their lot in life, it was this Samaritan woman. But when Jesus entered her life, everything changed. He took the initiative and spoke to her first, uncommon for a man to do in that culture. In the same way, He reaches out to us long before we reach toward Him. He looked at her as a person on the basis of her potential—not her past or even her present circumstances. Most importantly, He offered her a living water that would satisfy the emptiness and longing of her soul, a drink of water that would provide renewal for her parched soul and life.

Whatever troubles you're facing in life, be assured that today Jesus is offering you the same living water that He once offered a Samaritan woman on a hot, dusty day.

God's Promises for Tired Days

God will...

Give you rest from times of trouble
You give them relief from troubled times.

PSALM 94:13 NLT

Restore your joy
You changed my sorrow into dancing.
You took away my clothes of sadness,
and clothed me in happiness.

PSALM 30:11

Reward you with happiness
A good person can look forward to happiness.

PROVERBS 10:28

Enable you to have fun
God richly gives us everything to enjoy.

1 TIMOTHY 6:17

Renew your strength
*He gives strength to those who are tired
and more power to those who are weak.*

ISAIAH 40:29

Lighten your burdens
*Give your worries to the Lord,
and he will take care of you.
He will never let good people down.*

PSALM 55:22

A Prayer of Wonder and Thanksgiving

Heavenly Father,

*You have not created and redeemed me to live a dull,
gray, joyless, plodding life. Oh yes, I know you want
me to be sober-minded, to be true to my vows, but you
don't want me to take life or myself so seriously that
joy and laughter are squeezed from my soul.*

*Thank You for creating a world filled with wonder
and delight. Thank You for family and friends that
make my life so rich. Thank You that you want me
to find pleasure in following Your will and ways.*

*I am so thankful and blessed to join the celebration
You have created for our enjoyment.*

Acknowledgements

Meet the Pick-Me-Ups team

MARK GILROY
COMMUNICATIONS

Mark Gilroy, founder and president of Mark Gilroy Communications, Inc., has long served the publishing industry in a variety of editorial, marketing, and management roles. Jessica Inman, managing editor, is a freelance writer and editor. You can visit Mark Gilroy Communications at www.markgilroy.com.

Thinkpen Design, LLC is a leading graphic design firm for the Christian publishing and gift market. Under the leadership of design veteran Greg Jackson, Thinkpen specializes in product design creating gift books, greeting card lines, and gifts. Visit Thinkpen on the web at www.thinkpendesign.com.

ALSO AVAILABLE FROM THE PICK-ME-UP SERIES:

If you enjoyed *The Rainy Day Book*,
you're sure to love *The Bad Hair Day Book*.